Tales From the Gator Swamp

by
Jack Hairston

SPORTS PUBLISHING L.L.C.
WWW.SPORTSPUBLISHINGLLC.COM

Director of Production: Susan M. Moyer
Dustjacket and photo insert design: Christina Cary

ISBN: 1-58261-343-5

SPORTS PUBLISHING L.L.C.
www.sportspublishingllc.com

Printed in the United States.

To my late wife, Marjorie, who was my best friend for 47 years,
my conscience and my inspiration.
Without her and her love, I wouldn't have been much.

———————————————————

Acknowledgments

When I started work on this book, I thought the Gator football players would help me. They did so much more than that. Some drove to Gainesville to tell me their stories and give me their photographs, and many more made their contributions by phone or mail, others over lunch. Some of the contributors who went far beyond the call of duty and friendship were Red Mitchum, Frank Dempsey, Ed Kensler, Hill Brannon, Maurice Edmonds, Dick Pace, Dock Luckie, Dr. Robert Cade and the Gator athletic department's longtime communications ace, Norm Carlson. Scott Mitchum also helped with a wide collection of photos.

As always, my family was supportive. Daughters Beth Siegel and Martha Jost, sons-in-law Jeff Siegel and Paul Jost and grandsons Josh and Ben Siegel, Jacob and Jackson Jost.

Everyone I came in contact with at Sports Publishing was a pleasure to work with. My English teachers from my school days, Dixie Lou Armes, Mariah Butler and Thelma Moody, earned my thanks long ago. Thanks also to Joe Livingston, the editor who brought me to Florida 44 years ago, and to Sam Butz and Ed Johnson, editors who made most of my years in Florida happy ones. And to my two newspaper mentors from long ago, Carl Walters and Hap Glaudi. And to my first coach, who taught me important lessons about life many years ago, Joe Green, who'll turn 99 years of age in October and still has one of the sharpest minds I know.

And thanks are due to all the Gator football players who participated in the book and to all my friends and associates, particularly Marilyn Lowe, who assisted me greatly with the book in numerous ways.

Thanks to everyone who helped make the book become a reality.

Contents

Foreword

We are the boys of ol' Florida,
F-l-o-r-i-d-a
Where the girls are the fairest, the boys are the squarest,
Of any ol' place that I know . . . oh . . .

University of Florida football, starting in the 1990s, has consistently been of the championship variety, but the game has been played by the Gators since the first year of the university in 1906. There were near-miss championships as far back as 1954, actually back even to 1928 when the Gators were in the old Southern Conference. While the Gators weren't always outstanding, history indicates that the game was always embraced with a lot of enthusiasm by the players, students and fans. Many years there were more defeats than victories, but the Gators kept coming back, and so did their fans.

The 44 years I've been around Gator football, the typical Gator fan will complain bitterly about each defeat, sometimes putting the blame on the officials, more often putting it on the coaches. But the next game he'll be back, cheering the Gators as loudly as ever and contemplating a great Gator victory. Gator fans have been criticized many times over the years, but I've usually felt they were more loyal than those of any of the other schools I'd been close to.

The Gators and their fans have always w-a-n-t-e-d to be football champions. Like the courageous old battered and scarred knight of "The Impossible Dream," they never gave up their quest.

After 85 years of often heartbreaking pursuit, the Gators became champions in 1991. But during all those years that they were tattered also-rans, there was always an unusual spirit, a strong strand of humor, that ran through more Gators than anyone would expect. Soon after I arrived in Florida as a young sports writer in 1957, I realized the depth of that humor. How else could one of the nation's most powerful football traditions find a large part of its beginning in an 0-9 season? The players on that winless 1946 team labeled themselves "The Golden Era," and they've been having reunions each year for 40 odd years. I've been around a few teams that went through winless seasons, and the players on those teams usually have terrible memories of the year and have little interest in the subject even being brought up, much less having it toasted 50 years later.

The first time I was around a Florida Gator Golden Era celebration, I thought they were joking, and I asked several of the attendees what their rationale was. One of the ex-players, perhaps Jimmy Kynes or Marcelino Huerta, explained: "We feel like this was the time that the University of Florida first decided to seek real success in football. Over the years this group has stuck together, and we've been able to contribute to the University of Florida and to Gator football. We're an outspoken group and we love our alma mater.

"We didn't have many outstanding players in the Golden Era the 1940s, but a high percentage of this group has been very successful in life. We didn't win in football, but most of us have been winners in life, and that's contributed to the image of the University of Florida. It may be unique, but in our own way we helped Gator football get moving in the right direction."

In 1990, Steve Spurrier became Gator head coach and nicknamed Florida Field: The Swamp. It has become one of the most feared stadiums in America.

1

The Gator Ambassador

The name Red Mitchum will be connected with several stories in this book. If that wasn't so, it would mean that the researcher hadn't done a thorough job. William "Red" Mitchum finished as a 6-foot-3, 230-pound offensive tackle from Gadsden, Alabama, who was on the Florida teams of '48, '49, '50 and '51. He was a first teamer most of his last two seasons, just before the Gators had their first bowl team in 1952.

Not an award-winning football player, Red now has numerous trophies, plaques and proclamations citing him as "Gator Ambassador," "Most Valuable Gator Graduate," "Honorary Florida Sheriff," and on and on. He was the first UF student to serve as master of ceremonies of Gator Growl, the school's huge pep rally the night before Homecoming (the crowd has often exceeded 80,000).

Since leaving school, Red has spoken all over the nation, including an appearance at the Washington Press Club.

Mitchum's No. 1 foil on the UF football team was Curtis King, a fellow tackle who had a distinctive Southern drawl that sounded something like Gomer Pyle.

One day during a scrimmage at practice, offensive line coach John Eibner berated King for missing a block on a passing play. "You've GOT to make that cover block, or the quarterback is going to be killed," Eibner heatedly told King. "Now do it right!"

Eibner wheeled and walked away, and Mitchum, standing behind King, called out in his best Curtis King imitation: "Don't care if I EVER make that block, Coach. And I hate your guts!" Eibner, a former University of Kentucky All-America tackle, wheeled and started toward King, who shouted, "That wasn't me, Coach. That was Red Mitchum."

Eibner, realizing he'd been had, joined the players in a hearty laugh.

At the Auburn game one year, Mitchum and his roommate were placed in a room next door to Curtis and his roommate. Returning to his room after dinner, Mitchum knocked on King's door and shouted in his Curtis King voice: "Let me in." Curtis answered from

Red Mitchum (left) and Curtis King. (Photo courtesy of Scott Mitchum)

inside, "Who is that?" "I'm Curtis King," Mitchum replied through the door. "No, you're not!" was King's reply. "I'm Curtis King."

Mitchum shouted back, "I'm Curtis King. Honest!" A few moments later, King unlocked the door and took a look for himself. "Oh, Red," King said, clapping his hands, "you had me going for awhile there. I didn't know whether I was inside or outside! Then I figured it out. I was SURE I was on the inside, so I began to suspect somebody else was on the outside. And I was right!"

Red passes on this Curtis story, which he got from another Golden Era Gator, Jack Nichols, former mayor of Niceville, Florida.

Said Nichols: "The year after I graduated, I came back to Gainesville for a football game, and Curtis got me a date with a girl from near Gainesville who was studying karate. And she was built like Art Wright, the nose guard on our football team. You could tell she was real strong.

"After the game, the four of us drove out to the Millhopper (a sinkhole a few miles outside Gainesville) and parked. I was afraid my date might break my neck with a karate chop, so I didn't try anything. I heard a voice coming out of the backseat, and Curtis's date said, 'I know I stimulate you physically, but do I arouse you intellectually also?'

"Curtis said in his long drawl, 'Dadgum right. My brain is hard as a rock.'"

Curtis was manager of the Fort Pierce Airport for many years, and the city named the road to the airport Curtis King Boulevard. At a Florida Sheriffs Association banquet attended by both Mitchum and King, someone asked King if he was ever offended that Mitchum made fun of him in many stories. "Gracious, no," King said. "What he's done is made me famous. Why wouldn't I like that?"

Bob Woodruff was the Gator football coach who got the most mileage out of Red, although Mitchum won no honors as an All-SEC player. In the '60s, a football double header was played in Jackson, Mississippi, one Saturday, matching Ole Miss vs. Tennessee, Mississippi State vs. LSU. A Friday night dinner was staged for coaches and officials of all four teams, and Mitchum was hired to be the speaker.

Woodruff, then Tennessee AD, was asked to say a few words. He had coached both Mitchum and Barney Poole, who was also present and was the manager of Jackson Memorial Stadium. Poole had been an All-America end at West Point and Ole Miss, and Woodruff had been one of the line coaches at West Point.

"Being here with two of my former players reminds me of how much they have in common," Woodruff said. "Barney Poole was the absolute best player I ever coached, and Red Mitchum was the absolute worst player I ever coached."

Mitchum laughed as loudly as anyone at Woodruff's comment. But let's move away from Red for a while. You'll hear more from him in this book from time to time.

2

Bull York, Gator Poet

Bull York, a 1952 Gator letterman, was frustrated by the questions on an examination, and he wrote across the bottom of his paper, "Roses are red, violets are blue. Professor, if you wrote this paper, you're crazy too."

York was called into Woodruff's office the next day, and the Gator coach-athletic director told him, "Bull, the professor had complained about this. He said you wrote this thing across the bottom of your test paper and turned it in. Why in the world would you do that?"

York protested, "Coach, I didn't mean to put that on the paper I was going to turn in. I wrote the poem, but I thought I'd written on a piece of scratch paper. I didn't mean to turn it in."

Woodruff thought for a while, then said, "Bull, I believe you on this matter."

Bull, flabbergasted, said, "YOU DO?"

Haywood Sullivan, later the part owner and top executive officer of the Boston Red Sox baseball team, was the Gators' star quarterback as a sophomore and junior. Some of his teammates swore he was better than 1966 Heisman Trophy winner Steve Spurrier. Between his junior and senior seasons, he was offered a $45,000 bonus to sign a baseball contract with the Red Sox. Woodruff hoped to talk Sullivan into turning down the bonus and playing his final season (1952) for the Gators, an understandable hope on Woodruff's part.

The Gator coach decided to enlist Bill Terry, a Jacksonville automobile dealer and a Hall of Fame baseball player to help him persuade Sullivan to turn down the baseball offer. Woodruff phoned Terry to set up an appointment, but he didn't tell Terry what he wanted him to tell Sullivan.

Terry, who was as straight a shooter as I ever crossed paths with, said, "Woodruff and Sullivan came into my office and sat down. They explained all about the offer from the Red Sox. Then I asked Sullivan, 'Let me understand this. You get $45,000, and you get to keep it, even if you never get a hit for the Red Sox, even if you never get a hit in minor league baseball?' Sullivan said, 'That's right, Mr. Terry.' I said, 'Boy, what are waiting on?' Sullivan thanked me, and Woodruff looked kind of stunned, and they got up and walked out."

The story had a pretty happy ending. The Gator football team had an 8-3 season that year, including their first bowl game, but it was without Sullivan. The ex-Gator quarterback played some in the majors and managed in the majors before he became the Red Sox top executive and part owner, and he eventually retired from baseball as a multimillionaire.

Red Mitchum has been guest speaker at the annual football banquet of every Southeastern Conference school except Kentucky. On one of three appearances at the University of Georgia's football banquet, Mitchum told a story that upset some of the Georgia bigwigs. Mitchum took the name of one of Georgia's best and biggest linemen—let's call him "Jones"—and said one of Jones' teachers had told Red that he'd asked Jones in class who tore down the walls of Jericho, and Jones had answered, "I didn't do it, and anybody who says I did is a damned liar!"

Mitchum's story continued: "I thought it was funny, so when I bumped into Vince Dooley (Georgia's football coach) later this afternoon, I told him the teacher's story, and Vince said, 'I believe him, Red. If Jones said he didn't do it, that's good enough for me. We're sure not going to discipline him on that accusation unless we're given proof.' Then tonight before the banquet started, I was introduced to y'all's president, and I told him what Jones had said and what Vince had said. I thought they were funny. The president got sort of red in the face, and he said, 'I'll just say this: If Jones DID do it, the University of Georgia will be glad to pay for whatever the damage was.'"

3

Gators Reach Rose Bowl

Marcelino Huerta was a successful football coach and was in the same class with Red Mitchum as a character-humorist. Huerta was from Tampa's Spanish community, Ybor City, and he was known to almost everyone as "Chelo" (rhymes with jello).

The first night I heard him speak, he said from the dais, "When I got out of high school, the United States was having a lot of trouble in World War II. The U.S. asked me if I'd be a pilot for them, and I said yes, and I went on to win the war for them. After I got out of the service, the University of Florida contacted me and said, 'We want to go to the Rose Bowl. Will you help take us there?' I said, 'Sure, I'll take you there.'

"The first year at Florida we were 0-9, but when I lettered at guard the next three seasons, '47, '48 and '49, we were a lot better. Our best record was in '48. We were 5-5 that year. We had a lotta tough breaks.

But Florida made it to the Rose Bowl two years after I left. You can look it up. The Gators played Loyola of Los Angeles in the Rose Bowl on October 6, 1951 and beat 'em, 40-7."

Huerta coached winning teams at the University of Tampa, Wichita State and Parsons College. He was elected to the Florida Sports Hall of Fame, and before his induction at a ceremony at Cypress Gardens, I asked him what year he played his last game. "Officially it was 1949 for Florida," Huerta said, "but actually while I was coaching Tampa I played a bunch of games with them. I played almost every game out of town because we didn't have any fans who went to our road games. In the mid-'50s when I was in my early 30s, I was still playing in the road games.

"We played the University of Miami. Andy Gustafson was Miami's coach, and he'd called me a few days before the game and explained that the halftime entertainment was going to be 35 minutes instead of 20 minutes, and he wanted me to know ahead of time and keep my team in the dressing room about 15 extra minutes.

"Well, at the half we were getting killed, and I was at the blackboard, dirt smeared all over my face and my uniform, and I had a piece of chalk in one hand and a lit cigar in the other, diagramming stuff for my players. Part of the halftime show had been canceled at the last minute for some reason, and Gustafson figured he'd better tell me himself so I would know to get back out on the field after 20 minutes instead of 35. He walked into our dressing room, and there I stood at the blackboard, all grimy and puffing on that cigar. Gustafson took one look and said, 'Something funny is going on here!' I said, 'Coach, look at the scoreboard. You're beating us 35-0. What difference does it make if I play?' So Gus told me about the halftime change and walked out, and I never heard any more about it.

"I didn't play in many games after that, but Sam Bailey, my only assistant coach, played in the road games for several more years. Sam was about 35 years old and played end for us on the road. We were playing Austin-Peay up in Tennessee one night, and Sam got his leg broken. We traveled by bus, and we couldn't leave anybody at Austin Peay. That bus wasn't going to leave until Sam got a cast on his leg. We won the game, and after the players showered and dressed we took the bus and the players to the hospital to pick up Sam.

"I was watching the doctor finish fixing Sam up when a couple of the players walked in, and one said, 'How're you doing, Coach?' The doctor looked at Sam and said, 'I thought you were a player!' I said, 'He is a player, Doc. As you can see, he looks a lot older than he is, and the other players started calling him Coach.' We got out of that OK, but I never could talk Sam into playing in any more games."

Gene Ellenson was the Gators' defensive coordinator for eight of the 10 years he was on the staff (1960-69). He was outstanding and was the best psychologist on the staff. He badgered Coach Ray Graves until he named Ellenson "official coach of squad morale."

Ellenson took his job seriously, and he often spurred the players into a ferocious mood.

In 1963 the Gators had gotten off to a slow start, losing to Georgia Tech, tying Mississippi State and squeaking past Richmond, 35-28. A few Gator fans shouted insults at Graves and the Gators as they came off the field after the slim victory over Richmond. Next up for the Gators was a game with mighty Alabama in Tuscaloosa. Bear Bryant's team had never lost a game in Tuscaloosa, and they finished Bryant's term with just two home losses in 25 years. No one expected Florida to even make a contest of it with the Crimson Tide.

But Ellenson, who had distinguished himself as an infantry lieutenant under Gen. George Patton during the Battle of the Bulge, had been in tougher spots, and he wasn't going to give Alabama anything without them having to work for it.

Ellenson came up with the idea and told Graves about his plan: At a practice early in the week before the Alabama game, a plane would swoop low over the Gators and rain down on them a couple of hundred circulars. At the practice, in accordance with Ellenson's plan, the plane swooped down over the field. "Look, men!" Graves shouted. "A plane!" When the circulars started drifting down, Ellenson said, "Men, get those circulars! Let's see what they say!"

The players grabbed several of the circulars and read the message: "To the Gator Football Team: We are through supporting such an inept and gutless football team. We're not going to any more of your games. (Signed) THE GATOR ALUMNI."

Ray Graves and his Gators celebrating victory over Alabama.
(Photo courtesy of University of Florida Sports Information)

Graves, Ellenson and many of the players shook their fists at the plane and shouted a lot of profanities, plus a few cries of "We'll show you!" The rest of the week, Graves and Ellenson kept telling the players that this may be the most important game in Gator football history, with the disloyal alumni ready to shut off support of the Gators.

Somehow the Florida sportswriters got caught up in the squad's anger (naturally, the media had been critical of the Gators' early-season performances), and the team leaders asked Graves to bar the media from the dressing room after the Saturday game. They must have been eloquent in their arguments, because Graves and Ellenson, both of whom had excellent relationships with the sportswriters, agreed to keep them out.

Saturday the Gators attacked Alabama with a vengeance. Florida held a 10-0 lead with about two minutes to play in the fourth quarter. Alabama scored a TD, but the Tide's onside kickoff failed, and the Gators had won an upset that shook the nation.

The players insisted on barring the sportswriters from the dressing room, to the dismay of Graves and Ellenson, who didn't want maximum coverage of the great Gator victory to be sidetracked in any way. Graves told the media that this was the wish of the players, but he and Ellenson returned to the dressing room and persuaded several of the key players to come outside to talk to the media. By the following game, everyone had put all the turmoil aside, and things were back to normal in the Gator Nation.

The "alumni" plane with the circulars was topped six years later. The week before the 1969 Florida-FSU game, Ellenson outdid himself as a master psychologist. The Gators were 2-0 going into a home game against FSU, and the greatest firepower of the Gators had been the passing combination of John Reaves to Carlos Alvarez, a pair of sensational sophomores.

The Sunday prior to the game Ellenson took a Gator helmet and had Reaves' number seven painted on it. Then he took a Seminole hatchet and smashed it into the top of the helmet. He put the helmet-and-hatchet into a box and included a note that said: "This is what we're going to do to your fancy quarterback Saturday. He's going to be a dead Gator. (Signed) The FSU Defensive Line."

Ellenson addressed the box to: "The Gator Offensive Line, Yon Hall, University of Florida, Gainesville, Florida." Covering every detail, Ellenson gave the package to a Gator manager and directed him to drive to Tallahassee Monday morning to mail it. That's where the elaborate plan sprung a leak. The manager had a conflict of some kind and decided to mail it at the University of Florida Post Office in Gainesville.

When the package arrived at Yon Hall, the Gator offensive linemen opened it and absorbed its contents just as Ellenson had planned. They didn't notice the Gainesville postmark, and they were in a rage all week. Jimmy Haynes, in his first year as Gator offensive line coach, requested his players to spend extra time in the film room, studying those cursed Seminole defensive linemen.

Skip Amelung, a 245-pound offensive guard, wasn't a consistent viewer of films of the opponent, but he was reminded that he was playing in front of FSU's best defensive lineman, so he watched a film of the Seminoles. He got up to depart after one viewing, and the coaches reminded him of everything at stake. "It's all right," Amelung said. "I've seen enough and heard enough. That guy will not make a tackle Saturday. I guarantee it."

And he didn't make a tackle, and Reaves and Alvarez had a big day, and Reaves didn't get tackled a single time. Florida won, 21-6.

In case anyone thinks the Florida players weren't very smart to be bamboozled as they were by Ellenson, remember that football is an emotional game, and players sometimes will accept whatever is handed to them as motivation. . . and sometimes will go along with the moment, even if they smell a dead fish. Players will embrace a cause with all their hearts, even if they saw Captain Jack flying the "alumni" plane or saw a Gainesville postmark on the helmet-hatchet package mailed by "the FSU defensive line."

4

Hardest PAT Ever

John Piombo was a Gator end in 1938-39-40 and won a place in the hearts of many Gators by running a blocked punt for a touchdown against Georgia Tech to contribute to a 16-7 Gator triumph in 1940. He was an outstanding automobile salesman for many years in Jacksonville (he was good enough to sell me an Edsel in 1958 when I went into the store seeking a Mercury; Edsels dropped totally out of the market a few months later). But Piombo, now living in retirement in Jacksonville, has a memory from that game different from his touchdown.

"When Tech scored its touchdown," Piombo said, "and went back to kick the extra point, the center snapped the ball over the kicker's head, back about to midfield. The kicker ran back, picked it up and started running with it. He ran a ways and then threw a forward pass to a teammate. The teammate ran a distance, and he was still behind the line of scrimmage, so it was legal for him to throw another forward pass. He threw the ball to another teammate, who caught it and ran across the goal for the extra point. The Associated Press the next day called it 'the hardest earned point in the history of football.' "

The play sounds something like a forerunner to the California-Stanford play many years later when California lateraled the ball seven or eight times on a last-minute kickoff return and wound up the play running the winning touchdown through the Stanford band, which had marched onto the field while California was executing the weird play.

The Forrester twins, David and Dennis, were a pair of Gator offensive linemen out of Santa Fe High in 1975-76-77, each a first-team player, David at guard and Dennis at tackle. David now lives in Lake Wales and provided his most humorous moment as a Gator, which happened the night before the Gators' 1977 game against Auburn in Auburn: "It all began with our evening flight to Montgomery, Ala. During the flight I was seated next to (center) Mark Totten (note: Totten, right at 6-feet-6 and 300 pounds, was believed to be the largest Gator player ever at that time). We occupied seats near mid plane, with Mark seated next to the window.

"The flight proved uneventful, and we landed at Montgomery just after dark. As usual we taxied to a point near the terminal where buses were scheduled to arrive and transport us to our hotel for the evening.

Mark and I remained seated while other players and coaches began to disembark from the aircraft.

"While seated, I was looking out the window to see if the buses had arrived. I could see the buses approaching the plane, escorted by several Alabama Highway Patrol cars. As was routine at that time, the buses approached the plane, with the lead bus parking parallel to the plane. The action started as the second bus arrived, the driver of which had decided to park between the plane and the first bus. This proved to be a poor decision, because there was not enough room between the first bus and the wing of the plane.

"As the bus moved forward, it struck the wing of the plane near the bus's windshield below the destination sign. The speed and force was enough to cut through six to eight windows on the bus and to move the plane four to five feet before stopping. I remember seeing players and coaches falling within the plane. I was later told several players fell down the stairs while exiting the plane.

"During all this, I remember seeing an Alabama Highway Patrol officer standing in front of the bus, pointing his finger at the driver. I remember thinking: 'No way is Mark going to fit through the emergency window exit.' Luckily, there was no fire or serious injuries.

"As you might imagine, the rest of the trip followed a similar course, and Auburn defeated us the following day (Auburn 29, Florida 14)."

Ronnie "Tarzan" Slack (UF letterman, '58-59-60) and Jim Beaver (UF letterman, 1959-60-61) were the Gators' best tackles in '60 as Ray Graves' team moved toward a Gator Bowl date. The tackles were pals from West Palm Beach and both were in the school of administration, majoring in restaurant management. Slack provided this story, via the column of my old friend and staffmate Darrell Simmons of the *Atlanta Journal* sports department.

Simmons wrote: "Players, usually engineering majors, were excused from practice on afternoons they had labs. During one practice, head defensive coach Gene Ellenson went to Graves and complained, 'My two best tackles, Beaver and Slack, are missing.'

"Graves said, 'It's OK, Gene, they've got a lab today.' Ellenson started walking away, stopped and with a puzzled look, said, 'A lab in restaurant management?' Graves said, 'Yeah, that's right. I think they're learning to make a Waldorf salad.' Purely a matter of academics superseding athletics."

Tom Abdelnour, nicknamed "The Sheik," was a 5-foot-8, 190-pound linebacker who was a standout on the '69 Gator team that went 9-1-1, including a victory over SEC champion Tennessee in the Gator Bowl. Now a professor at the University of Michigan, Abdelnour provides this contribution to Gator humor:

"As you know, I lettered from 1967 to 1969 and was captain of the Gators along with (All-SEC offensive tackle) Mac Steen. My linebacker coach was Gene Ellenson, a man loved by all Gators who knew him.

"Let me share a few stories. As you know, some of these stories have that 'you had to be there' component to appreciate the entire humor in the story. The stories below are very true and are my best recollection.

"In the summer of 1965 I played in the North vs. South High School All-Star game in Gainesville. I played for the South, and we won a hard-fought game. After the game, I went out celebrating with two of my teammates, Bill Trout and Chuck Eson. We had been drinking far too much beer and were considering calling it an evening late that night. I was driving and spotted a three-foot alligator in the road. I stopped the car and got out to take a closer look. I decided to capture the gator by using my belt as a loop. After looping the gator around the neck, I threw him in the trunk of the car. The three of us decided to take the gator to one of the dorms (as we laughed out of control) to have a little fun. We carried the gator into the dorm only to find out there was no one in the dorm!

"We were about to leave when we heard a shower running in one of the bathrooms. We walked quietly into the bathroom and tossed the gator into the shower! The instant the gator got past the shower curtain the guy in the shower leaped out of the shower screaming as loud as he could! Moments later a policeman stepped into the bathroom and demanded an explanation.

"Bill Trout picked up the gator and shoved it into the face of the policeman, yelling, 'Here you go, officer! I don't want this gator anymore!' The police officer was nice enough not to get mad at us. He made us take it back to the closest lake. I did not meet the young man who jumped out of the shower until a year later. It was Mac Steen! We later became the cocaptains of the Gators in 1969."

"My next story. . . I cannot recall which game, but the story occurs in 1968 or 1969. We were playing some team, and Coach Ellenson had it in his mind that we were going to blitz the opponent's quarterback. It seemed like every defensive play Gene would signal to me was to call a blitz. Over and over again, Gene would signal me to call a blitz, and blitz was what I called. We continued our blitzing, but we did not seem to get to the quarterback. I was getting frustrated in addition to getting creamed on every play by a guy at least 70 pounds bigger than me.

"Gene signaled me yet another blitz! I looked at Gene as if to say, 'No, I am not going to call another blitz.' I called another defense; it was not a blitz. I made the tackle on the play. As I got up, I noticed Mike Palahach come running on the field to substitute for me. I ran off the field as quick as I could. Gene was at the sideline waiting for me. He had that look in his eye, and I knew I had done something wrong.

"Gene grabbed me by my jersey and in his deepest and angriest voice he said, 'Sheik, I ain't the pitcher, and you ain't the catcher! Don't ever call off my signal again!' He scared me so bad I ran back on the field just to get away from him! . . .

"P.S.: And then there was the day Coach Don Brown was trying to draw up some defensive plays on the chalkboard. Don was a very excitable guy. I guess he got a little carried away drawing on the chalkboard and explaining the plays to us. He grabbed his cigarette lighter, stuck a cigarette in his mouth and began to light the cigarette. The only problem was he had grabbed a piece of chalk in lieu of his cigarette! Steve Tannen (cornerback) was the first to notice this and yelled out, 'Coach, you're trying to smoke the chalk!'"

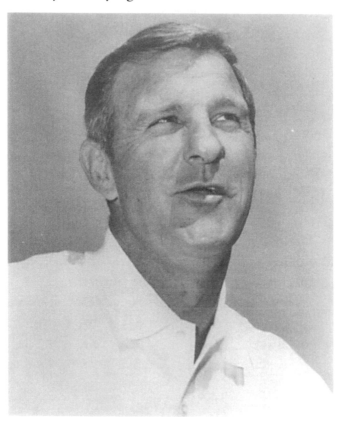

Assistant Coach Don Brown (Photo courtesy of University of Florida Sports Information)

5

Attack on Albert

Abdelnour's Gator story reminds me of a story Dick Skelly confirmed to me recently about the most famous football player-alligator mascot story in Gator history. Three Gator football lettermen, halfbacks Skelly and Bob Hoover and end-place kicker Billy Cash, decided one spring night that they would enter the cage of Gator mascot Albert as a prank. The large gator was kept in a pen on campus at that time, and this story is the main reason a live mascot is no longer kept on campus.

On a dare from some coeds, the three gridders decided they'd enter Albert's cage and cut off a small piece of his tail to prove they'd been in the cage. In the dark of night Skelly and Hoover entered the cage (Cash stayed outside as the lookout). Skelly, who had brought on the mission a Boy Scout hatchet with his name carved into the handle, took several whacks at Albert's tail. Albert responded with a ferocious roar. Hoover fled the cage, and Skelly took another whack at Albert's tail, then fled, too, leaving his hatchet inside the cage. But the last whack had produced a small piece of Albert's tail, which Skelly carried with him as he reached safety.

A campus police officer drove up, and the players departed in haste. Skelly began fretting about having left his hatchet in the cage, and he returned to the scene of the crime to see if anything could be done about retrieving the hatchet. The policeman had somehow gotten possession of the hatchet, and he was sharing the information with several passersby that the name "Skelly" was on the hatchet's handle. One of the students at the scene saw Skelly, pointed at him and yelled, "There he is!"

Skelly made no resistance as the policeman arrested him, and Hoover and Cash soon "surrendered" and admitted their roles in the fiasco. The players didn't expect much to come of the incident, but several newspapers reported the story, and soon it was the talk of the campus. Some people demanded that all three be suspended from the football team, but the football coaches came to the players' defense.

Each of the three had contributed to the 1960 team the previous fall as sophomores, Hoover as a first-team halfback, Cash as a kicker whose record-breaking field goal had beaten LSU in Baton Rouge, Skelly as a halfback who was playing well until a knee injury cut him down in the season's third game.

In the spring of '61 Skelly and Hoover were the first-team halfbacks, and the coaches had Skelly, a 210-pounder with speed, tabbed as likely to be the key man of the offense. Skelly had been the key player on the '59 Gator freshman team that posted a perfect record.

The university disciplinary committee decided to rule Skelly ineligible for one season, but Hoover and Cash were spared and played their remaining two seasons, Hoover as a starter. Skelly returned to the team in '62 but was bothered by the knee injury. He played in three games and was banished from the team by the coaches for skipping several treatment sessions.

Skelly was drafted by the New York Giants of the National Football League. Peahead Walker, the colorful scout who had recommended him to the Giants, was asked about the recommendation. "Easy decision," Walker said. "His problem at Florida was alligators, and there ain't no alligators in New York."

But the knee was still a problem, and Skelly didn't stay long with the Giants.

"I wasn't one of the players who got a lot of applause from the fans," Red Mitchum, the former Gator offensive tackle, said once. "But one game in '50 or '51, we were third and goal on the 2-yard-line, and Coach Woodruff called me over. I thought he wanted me to go in with the next play, and I think that was it, but he was forgetful some time. He got me by the arm and said, 'Get in there.' Then he pulled me back. He said, 'Get in there,' two more times before he finally sent me in. He didn't give me any play to call.

"I came running to the huddle, and Sullivan (the quarterback), said, 'What did he say to call?' I said, 'All he said was, "Get in there." One of the other players said, 'What's the matter with you? I know he said more than that!' Sullivan said, 'I know Coach Woodruff, and I can believe that's all he said.' So Sully decided on the play without any help from the sideline, and we scored. As I trotted off the field, the Gator fans were cheering and shouting, and one of them yelled, 'Way to go, Red! You got the right play in!' I appreciated his encouragement, but I was getting credit for just saying, 'He said, "Get in there."

Steve O'Connell was an SEC championship middleweight boxer for the Gators in the '30s, was a Florida Supreme Court justice and was president of the university, 1967-73. He wrote from Tallahassee, where he lives in retirement: "I have searched my failing memory and can recall only one story that may fit your need. It is:

"Fergie Ferguson, a tall, rangy Florida end, dropped a pass he should have caught on the sideline where Florida students sat. As he turned after dropping the pass, a Gator student yelled, 'You bum, even I could have caught that pass.'

"Fergie walked toward the student and yelled back, 'If I had your big mouth, I could have caught that ball in it.'"

Fergie Ferguson was the Gators' second player to win All-America honors in 1941. He died of wounds suffered in World War II and is one of the Gators most talked about in complimentary terms by his peers.

6

The Culpeppers

Blair Culpepper is from one of those few families that could make a good case for being THE Family of Florida Gator Football. His father, Broward, was a UF grad and was for many years the executive director of the State Board of Regents, which at that time controlled all state-owned colleges in Florida.

Blair lettered two years at UF as a fullback (1957-58) and has been a bank president in Winter Park for many years. Bruce, Blair's brother, lettered three years at UF as a center ('60, '61, '62), was cocaptain of the '62 Gator Bowl team and has been a lawyer in Tallahassee for many years. Brad, son of Bruce, played for the Gators ('88 through '91), was an All-America defensive tackle in '91 and won the '91 Draddy Scholarship Trophy, presented annually by the National Football Foundation and College Hall of Fame to the nation's premier football scholar-athlete. Brad has been playing in the NFL since graduation.

Blair wrote: "I can think of a few incidents. Most have to do with Coach Bob Woodruff. In two-a-days before the 1956 season we would drag out to morning practice. It was always hot and humid. Some of my teammates would actually hide in the big stack of blocking dummies in the middle of the practice field, catching a few winks before we started. Coach Woodruff came out one morning and was poking around the dummies. He suddenly began blowing his whistle furiously. We all ran over in anticipation. To us the coach said, 'You guys are early. . . Manager, get this frog off the field.' . . .

"At Lexington (the Kentucky game), Coach Woodruff called me over. 'Culpepper, Culpepper, get in there and run. . . Never mind. Come back.' (A few plays later) 'Culpepper, get in there and run. . . Never mind. Never mind.' . . . (A few plays later) 'Get Culpepper out of there.' A few feet away from him on the sideline, I said, 'I'm over here, Coach. . . .'

"The 1956 season got off to a big start when Florida crushed Mississippi State 26-0 at Starkville. Joe Brodsky had his greatest day as a linebacker, returning two interceptions for touchdowns. The last interception was run back 100 yards, still an NCAA record. Brodsky ran out of gas at about the 15-yard-line and barely made it into the end zone. As he lay face down in the end zone he mumbled, 'Y'all are going to have to carry me to the bench. I can't get up.'"

Brad Culpepper (Photo courtesy of University of Florida Sports Information)

"The Gators went to their first bowl game after the 1952 season," Red Mitchum said, "the year after I graduated. A few years later they had a reunion of that Gator Bowl team, and Coach Woodruff asked me to be the guest speaker. He introduced me, and he presented me with a small plaque with a football helmet on it. The inscription read: 'Red Mitchum contributed more to that Gator Bowl team by graduating than J. "Pappa" Hall, who was voted Most Valuable Player in the game.'

"Everybody had a big laugh, and then Coach Woodruff gave me a real trophy three feet high. The inscription on that one read: 'To Red Mitchum, voted by his peers to be the Most Valuable Graduate of the University of Florida in the last 40 years. To Red Mitchum, Gator Ambassador.'"

Red remembers well the important dates joining him and the Gators. Out of Gasden, Alabama, he signed with the Gators in the summer of 1946, a 6-foot-2, 162-pound end. The draft was still on, even though World War II had ended in August, 1945. The Army offered a deal whereby potential draftees could volunteer, and they would be released from active duty after 18 months. Red and Angus Williams, later first-team quarterback and captain for the Gators, were two Gator players who grabbed the deal. The two were soon separated by the Army, but they wound up in a service football game—against each other—in Japan.

"That turned out to be a big break for me," Red said. "I was playing right end on defense, and on the first play, Angus called a naked rollout to my side. I nailed him, and his shoulder got dislocated. They took Angus to the hospital, so he only saw that one play in the game. When we were getting out of the service, Coach (Bear) Wolf asked Angus whether I was worth bringing back to play football, and Angus said, 'I played against him in a game, and he's a dadgum good end. He's really improved.'

"A guy in my outfit in the Army had talked to Coach Bud Wilkinson at Oklahoma about me, and Coach Wilkinson promised me a scholarship. Coach Wolf phoned me and tried to talk me into coming to Florida. What I remembered most about that summer of '46 under Coach Wolf was that he put us through nine weeks of two-a-days. Really. But he said Florida took me when nobody else wanted me, and he said, 'We'll give you the gym if you come here.' So I came back to Florida, but they never gave me anything. Still, it was the best thing that ever happened to me, next to being married to Grace for 50 years."

Bobby Ennis, former Gator manager, remembered the summer of '46 another way: "We didn't have TV then, and we didn't have enough money to go to the movies, so Red was our entertainment every night. He'd get outside Murphree Hall and play his matchbooks and sing and tell stories just like he does now."

"Florida signed me after the Army because Angus Williams said I was a good defensive end," Mitchum said. "Then Coach Woodruff came in as our coach in

'50, and he shifted me to offensive tackle. Angus was the quarterback and captain, and when he saw me at offensive tackle, he went to Woodruff and asked to be switched to defense. That's how good I was. Angus stayed at quarterback, but he's the one who said I invented the 'lookout block.' I'd try to block the tackle, and I'd miss, and I'd holler, 'Look out!' Made me real popular with all the backs."

When Red was a senior, Marshall Criser, later president of UF, was president of Blue Key, which puts on Gator Growl, commonly called the "world's largest pep rally." Criser asked Red after a football practice to MC Gator Growl, but Red declined. "I'd love to do it, but Coach Woodruff doesn't like us to do outside things during football season," Red explained. "He's always telling us, 'Think about the football game.' I'm just barely on the first team, and if he hears I'm going to MC Gator Growl, my days on the first team could be over.'"

Criser offered no protest, but two days later Red got a message to report to Coach Woodruff's office. He tried to figure out what he could possibly have done to get called in. "Woodruff told me to sit down," Red said, "and I knew I was REALLY in trouble. He said he'd heard that I had been asked to do Gator Growl. I said, 'Yes, sir, but I turned it down. I'm thinking only about football.' Woodruff said he wanted me to reconsider, and he said he could give me three good reasons. He said, 'One, it'll be an honor for the team to have a football player be the first student to MC Gator Growl. Two, it'll be good for recruiting for everyone to know a

Red Mitchum, Gator Growl MC (Photo courtesy of Scott Mitchum)

football player can say more than, "DUH!" And three, President J. Hillis Miller phoned me and said you WERE going to do it.'

"I laughed and said, 'That third reason is the real one, isn't it? The first two reasons really don't mean anything, do they?' 'They don't mean a damn thing,' Woodruff said. So I became the first student to MC Gator Growl."

Woodruff is in retirement now after 10 years as UF football coach and athletic director, followed by 22 years as athletic director at his alma mater, the University of Tennessee. Now 84 years old, Woodruff was phoned by Mitchum last summer. During the conversation, Woodruff couldn't recall one person Red brought up. "Coach, pretty soon you won't even be able to remember me," Red said. "Naw, Red," Woodruff said, "I'll always remember you. I know, though, there are people who go to psychiatrists and pay money to try to forget you."

7

Losing Frank Mordica

On a Southeastern Conference Skywriters tour in the mid-'70s, P. W. "Bear" Underwood, Auburn defensive line coach, provided the most entertaining recruiting story I'd ever heard. Underwood, about 5-9 and 250 pounds as a college player, had been a standout guard at Southern Mississippi and in the Canadian League, then worked his way up to head coach at Southern Mississippi, a job he filled for six years. He then served on the staffs of Vanderbilt and Auburn.

The story involved Vanderbilt and Florida both seeking to sign Frank Mordica, a fast 200-pound running back out of Tallahassee, between the seasons of 1974 and '75. Underwood represented Fred Pancoast's

Vandy staff in the pursuit of Mordica, while secondary coach Allen Trammell and assistant track coach Brooks Johnson represented Doug Dickey's Florida staff. Limits on the number of recruiters were different from present rules, and Johnson was able to assist Florida on a part-time basis, concentrating primarily on football players interested in track, as Mordica was.

"I was in Tallahassee to visit Mordica," Underwood said. "I went to his mother's house early in the after-

Allen Trammell (Photo courtesy of University of Florida Sports Information)

noon. Mordica wasn't home from school yet, and the boyfriend of Mrs. Mordica, who was a single mother, invited me in. Then Trammell and Johnson arrived, and the boyfriend invited them in, too. Johnson was one of the slickest-dressed recruiters I'd ever seen. He had on a silk suit and a silk shirt and a silk tie, with a gold stickpin. He was really slick.

"The boyfriend asked if he could get us something to drink, and we all said yes. He reached up in the cupboard and came out with a fifth of a cheap whiskey I'd never heard of. It was called Old Wilkins Family, or something like that. I think it sold for like a $1.50 a fifth, and the bottle was all beat up like it had been around a long time, and I could see why. Brooks Johnson looked at the bottle and said, 'Brother, do you put liquor like that in your stomach? I don't drink anything that costs less than $7.50 a fifth.'

"The boyfriend seemed a little embarrassed, and I reached over and took the fifth out of his hand, took the top off and raised the bottle to my lips and took a big swig. The stuff like to have taken my breath away, but I caught my breath, and I said to the boyfriend: 'This is plenty good enough for me!' Then I pointed at Brooks Johnson and said to the boyfriend, 'This man has insulted you in your own home. If I were you, I wouldn't put up with that.' The boyfriend looked hard at Johnson and said to him and Trammell, 'I'm going to have to ask you gentlemen to leave my home.' He made 'em leave. I wound up getting Mordica for Vanderbilt."

When I got back to Gainesville, I looked up Trammell, told him Underwood's story and asked him how much of it was true. Trammell turned a couple of shades of red and said, "Every word of that is true, Jack. The only thing he didn't include was that Brooks and I were out in the yard after the boyfriend asked us to leave. I was wondering what I'd done to be thrown out of the house and what I was going to tell Coach Dickey about not even getting to SEE Mordica. About that time Underwood came running out the door and threw up in the bushes in front of the house. That big swig of that liquor had gotten to him. But he did wind up getting his man. Mordica went to Vanderbilt."

In '78 Mordica set an SEC record that still stands when he rushed for 321 yards in 22 carries for Vanderbilt against Air Force—14.6 yards per pop. I never heard any more about Johnson recruiting football players, but he advanced to become head track coach at Southern Cal, and he was a member of the U.S. Olympic staff at the 1984 Olympic Games in Los Angeles.

Dale Van Sickel was the Gators' first All-America football player in 1928 as an end. He went to Hollywood as an actor but eventually switched to being a stunt man for the movies. He was an award winner in his field. The Gators went to Los Angeles in 1958 to play UCLA, going out on Wednesday before the Friday night game. Van Sickel and his wife came by the team hotel Thursday afternoon to visit the Gators for a while. Woodruff invited the Van Sickels and several sportswriters to his suite for drinks and conversation.

For a plane trip to the West Coast, someone had purchased 30 or 40 young alligators, varying in size from about a foot to about two feet. The two-footers were big enough and had enough teeth that you wouldn't want to offer your hand to one of them. When the plane landed in LA, the Gator football players were to deplane, each carrying one of the young alligators. The UCLA cheerleaders were greeting the plane, and the Gator players were to hand the alligators to the cheerleaders as friendship gifts. The cheerleaders had not been given this information.

It may have sounded like a good idea before the trip, but the way it turned out, no one was willing to say whose idea it was. First, when the alligators were presented, the UCLA cheerleaders shrieked, turned and ran for safety. When everything eventually calmed down, the cheerleaders were firm in their insistence that they would not accept their alligator gifts. Now the Gator party had 30 or 40 alligators on its hands, and no one had an immediate idea of what to do with them. With the media spotlight so bright on the Florida party, it wouldn't be a good idea to dump the alligators down the sewer or flush them down a toilet. The Society for the Prevention of Cruelty to Animals would have made the Gators their poster kids for the year.

Eventually the decision was made to donate the alligators to the Los Angeles Zoo, but there was enough red tape involved to prevent that transaction from happening for 24 hours. The Gator party was stuck with the alligators for one full day. Someone decided (I'll bet you it wasn't Margaret Woodruff, Bob's wife) that the best place to put the alligators was in Coach Woodruff's suite, because it was the largest area anyone in the party was staying in. Coach Woodruff, as always, was the good soldier, and the critters were all dumped into the tub in his bathroom.

They were still there the next afternoon during the visit of the Van Sickels and the sportswriters. By then, the alligators had begun crawling out of the tub, and it was an adventure every time anyone needed to use the bathroom. Also, every time the bathroom door was opened, the alligators would crawl through it and enter the area where Woodruff's guests were. Pretty soon almost everyone in the room had participated in picking up an alligator and dumping it back in the bathtub.

The larger alligators with the larger teeth sometimes crawled well into the room before anyone would volunteer to put them back in the bathroom. I was trying to interview Van Sickel and record the conversation between him and Woodruff, and it wasn't the least-stressful accomplishment of my career. By Friday, game day, the alligators had been taken to the zoo, and Woodruff's concentration could return to the game. (Florida beat UCLA, 21-14.)

8

Rhodes Scholar Gator

Bill Kynes was a second-generation Gator in one of those outstanding Gator families. His father, Jimmy, was an All-SEC center in the Golden Era. His brother, Jimbo, was first-team center for the Gators in '72 and '74, the latter team reaching the Sugar Bowl for the first time in UF history. Bill lettered at quarterback in '75 and '76 and was ticketed to be the first-team quarterback in '77. However, he received a Rhodes Scholarship to Oxford University in England and departed UF before the season rolled around. He was one of the top students at UF and had graduated in less than three years on campus.

Bill at first requested that his Rhodes Scholarship be delayed until 1978, but the Rhodes people told him he'd have to start it in '77 or forget about it. I'm sure there were some people who thought he should have turned down the Rhodes Scholarship, but not one person whom I talked to expressed that feeling. Bill is now a minister living in Annandale, Virginia.

I got an unconfirmed tip in 1977 that Bill was going to accept the Rhodes offer and skip his final season of football. I wanted to get that information confirmed by Bill. Jimbo was in law school at UF, and I phoned him that night in my search for Bill. Jimbo said, "Bill's different from most football players. If you look in the places where you might find Gator players, you'll never find him. If you want to find him tonight, I'd recommend you phone the University Library." That's where I found him, and he confirmed his impending departure.

Bill answered my recent request for a Gator story or two with this letter: "I'm not the best one to ask for funny stories. In my era, I think of Lee McGriff, Ralph Ortega, J.R. Richards and John Clifford as the premier story tellers. I mostly just listened and laughed. They especially told stories about assistant coach Jack Hall and tight end Ronnie Enclade—they were real characters. I will share one short one that comes to mind:

"On those hot, humid days early in the season, players were always trying to get out of practice, and I remember one player dragging up to our pre-practice meetings in the coaches' offices. He whined to Coach Jimmy Dunn (offensive coordinator), 'Coach, Coach, I can't go today. I think I got sickle-cell.' Coach Dunn was hardly sympathetic but played along: 'Well don't

Jimmy Dunn (Photo courtesy of University of Florida Sports Information)

get near me. Is that CONTAGIOUS?' The player replied, 'Sure it'll kill ya! . . .'

"I hate to mention it, but there was the time I was working as the athletic dormitory resident manager, and a senior football player asked me where the library was!"

(Well, better late than never.)

Wendell "Billy" Parker was a halfback and punter who lettered for the Gators ('46-47-48), back in the Golden Era. He was a longtime school administrator in Jacksonville and provides this: "Coach Bear Wolf told me the reason he used me as the Gator punter in '46 and '47 was I couldn't kick the football far enough to reach the safety; the opponent

Billy Parker didn't punt too far. (Photo courtesy of Billy Parker)

had no opportunity to run it back. We did a lot of so called coffin-corner kicks or 'be sure to kick it out-of-bounds' kicks in those days. We also punted on third down if we were behind the 50-yard-line in our own territory.

"The high 50- and 55-yard kicks of today were just unheard of then. Mine were usually low and rolled well. Fred Montsdeoca took over the kicking chores in '48 and '49 and did a great job."

The Gators were playing The Citadel in '50, and Jack Nichols provides this story: "Buford Long and I were the cornerbacks, and J. Pappa Hall was the safety.

The Citadel was getting ready to try a short field goal. Pappa was the NCAA high-jump champion, and I persuaded Buford and Pappa to go along with me on this idea I came up with. I wanted Pappa to jump up in front of the goal posts and catch the ball and run with it. Buford and I would block for him. I thought we'd catch Citadel off guard.

"Well, it worked. Pappa jumped up in front of the goal posts and caught the ball and ran 109 yards for a touchdown, the longest touchdown run in history. Buford and I each made two blocks on this long, winding run. However. . . clipping at The Citadel 30 nullified the touchdown and changed it to a 79-yard run. But we came that close to the longest run ever."

Bob Gilbert, a letterman halfback in '46 for the Gators, had been on the squad before World War II, and he used a true story from 1942 to assist in a highly unusual situation in November, 1944. Gilbert and a pair of his teammates were en route from Fort Myers to Gainesville for the start of fall practice in September, 1942. They decided to save a few bucks and jump a freight train in Tampa, headed for Jacksonville.

The box car they picked out, to their disappointment, proved to be a shipment of manure. The second bad break came when they reached Gainesville: The train didn't even pause in Gainesville and went roaring through the town at 50 miles an hour. The players couldn't jump off at that speed, so they stayed on the train. They realized eventually that the train wasn't going to stop until it reached Jacksonville. When the train reached Starke the next morning and slowed down just a tad, the players jumped off at intervals.

"We tore up our clothes on the jump," Gilbert said, "and we were bruised. . . and stinky. But we were a lot closer to Gainesville than we would have been in Jacksonville."

In November of '44, Gilbert was captured in Germany during the Battle of the Bulge.

"They put me and 39 other American prisoners in a box car to move us deeper into Germany," Gilbert said. "It was freezing, and it was a pretty miserable situation. As you might expect, morale was pretty low in that box car. But the situation reminded me of the box car I was stuck in back on my Florida trip two years before that, and I told that story to the other prisoners. They got to laughing about me and the other two Gator players, and it seemed to take everybody's mind off the mess we were in. At least it made the time pass a little faster. I never thought that box car story from Florida would ever be of any use to anybody, but it was to those prisoners. It perked them up."

Tommy "Red" Harrison was a standout tailback at Florida (1939-40-41) and held the UF career total offense record for 24 years (2,133 yards). He was an assistant coach two years at Vanderbilt and two years at UCLA, then went into the business end of radio broadcasting. He completed his career in New York as presi-

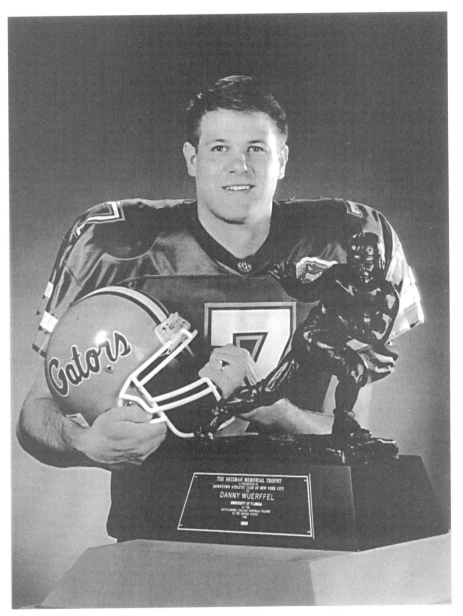

Danny Wuerffel, Gator Career Yardage Champion (Photo courtesy of University of Florida Sports Information)

dent of Blair Radio Representatives and now lives in retirement in Vero Beach at the age of 81.

Harrison wrote regarding this publication: "In 1966 I was asked by Carlos Proctor (ex-assistant coach at U of Florida) to attend a cookout he was having for the Gator football team during their spring practice. After I arrived there at his ranch he called Steve Spurrier over and said, 'Steve, I want you to meet Tommy "Red" Harrison. You broke his 24-year-old total offense record.' Steve said how glad he was to meet me and then said, 'No one told me I had broken your record.' As we turned away from each other, I said to my friend, 'I knew I held the record, but I didn't realize I held it for 24 years.'"

Spurrier's career total-offense record was 3,212 yards after his junior season, and he increased his numbers to 5,290 yards by the end of his senior season, but if you don't think 24 years is a long time for Harrison to hold the record, consider that no one has held it that long at UF since him. Spurrier's UF record for total offense lasted only five years and was broken by John Reaves. Reaves (7,283 yards) held the record for 21 years, and it has since been surpassed twice, first by Shane Matthews (9,241 yards, 1989-92) and then by Danny Wuerffel (10,500 yards, 1993-96).

9

Talbot's Survival

Randy Talbot was a three-year letterman at cornerback for the Gators (1972-73-74). He coached a short time at UF, then worked for the UF development department for several years, and now works (brace yourself) for the Florida State University development department.

He responds to a letter regarding this book: "It was late into two-a-days. We freshmen still had our names taped to the front of our helmets so the coaches could bark out with specificity who they wished to sacrifice for the moment. We were on Florida Field, and the announcement echoed throughout the stadium: 'Punt cover, punt cover . . . Freshmen DBs down here.' So off a handful of us trekked.

"Coach Lindy Infante motioned for us to gather around him at the 45-yard line. We could see the varsity punt cover team lining up facing us about 40 yards away. Infante informed us we were to catch the ball, run with it, and there were to be no fair catches. OK, that's simple. So I took my usual place near the back of the line. You see I wanted to watch this myself. I was curious to see just how this was going to work, since there were no other receiving personnel on the field except my fellow DBs, who were waiting in line.

"First DB up . . . the snap, the kick, a long, high, lazy spiral heading downfield, followed by 10 snorting, huffing and puffing, turf-pounding crazed cover fanatics, drawing a bead on the DB, who is watching the punt, zeroing in under its flight. He's got it . . . Ohhhhhh. That had to hurt. He never had a chance to run. He gets up slowly, a little stagger and a 'good job' from Infante.

"This goes on until it's my turn, and it's been ugly to watch. Poor little DBs are getting hammered. The snap, the kick, it's a high, lazy spiral. I look

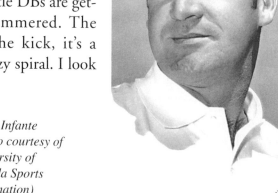

Lindy Infante (Photo courtesy of University of Florida Sports Information)

at the ball, glance down at the thundering stampede who are drawing a bead on me. I look skyward again, position myself and glance at the white of 20 eyes; I can feel their presence.

"Their pounding footsteps have caused the turf to vibrate, and I can feel it from my toes to my mouthpiece. I quickly locate the ball, take one last glance at my demise and signal a fair catch. I cradle the ball into my arms as I take a knee.

"For a brief moment, time stands still. I can hear birds singing, cars driving by on University Avenue. The thundering herd has stopped at my feet, broken down in a ready stance waiting for a fumble that does not materialize. They stare at me with wrinkled brow, spit and snot emanating from their breath, but no one dares to touch me. The serenity of the affair is broken by the bellowing of Coach Infante.

"'What the hell are you doing? I told you no fair catches. What's the matter with you? You're supposed to run, dammit! Now do it again, and do it right!' 'Yes, sir,' was my only response.

"I line up facing my sure demise, because the group who came down without the satisfaction of returning with a kill is now having to repeat the exercise without rest. The snap, the punt, a high, lazy spiral heading downfield, followed by those 20 eyes who are no longer white, but red with blind fury. I glance at the ball, then the angry hoard, the ball, the hoard, the ball, the hoard, the ball, signaling for a fair catch, whereupon I cradle my prize into my arms, taking a knee.

"I can feel the hot, stale breath and indignant stares of my upper classmates. Their disdain is real, but they dare not touch even my shoelace. The silence is broken by footsteps quickly crushing the stiff bristles of the artificial turf, stopping at my side, whereupon I feel, then see, a hand grab my face mask, wheeling my head to my would-be assailant. With eyes, nose and breath entering my being through my face mask all at the same time, I feel my head being pushed backwards, and the eyes, nose and breath scanning the front of my helmet for a name. Whereupon, having secured same, the trinity is back with a violent jerk forward.

"Talbot, didn't I tell you to catch the ball and run?' 'Yes, sir.' 'Didn't I tell you no fair catches?' 'Yes, sir.' 'Then what the hell's the matter with you? Don't you speak English?' That's one of their favorite lines. An awkward silence fills the air as the trinity waits for an answer. 'Coach, I would never do what you told me to do in a game, so why should I do it here?'

"There is a pause, then a look to the left, then the right and a smile crosses Coach Infante's face, in a hushed voice he says, 'Talbot, you're too smart, go to the back of the line.'"

It might have been difficult to predict that hot summer day, but Talbot finished his career as an All-SEC cornerback, and Infante finished his as head coach of the Green Bay Packers and the Indianapolis Colts of the NFL.

10

Bank Robbers 'R Us

One Gator gridder of long ago, who shall remain anonymous, had a few run-ins with the law. He was caught in the High Springs Bank one morning at 4:30 a.m. "What are you doing in here?" the law asked. "I just came in to cash a check," the Gator replied. The law didn't believe him.

One Gator volunteered this information about the burglar, and there was no pride in his voice: "He could have gotten away with both bank burglaries he was arrested for. The first one he was hiding under a desk, and the police didn't find him. But he heard the police leave, and he stood up. The trouble was one policeman was still there, investigating, and he saw him and arrested him. In the other one he got to his car, which was a fast car, and he took off, but he ran into a pond and got stuck, and the police caught up and arrested him as he was coming out of the pond."

Another bank in the area was burglarized on a Saturday night at the exact same time the Gators were playing the University of Miami in a football game at the Orange Bowl. When the Gators were en route home by train the next day, the train was stopped by the law. The Gator suspect was questioned about where he was the previous evening. He said he was playing in the football game in Miami. The authorities then questioned the Gator coaches, and only after the coaches confirmed the player's participation in the game was he dropped as a suspect.

Van Fletcher, a longtime prominent restaurant owner in Jacksonville, was a rabid supporter of the Gators, and he treated the players like royalty whenever they visited his Green Derby. A Gator player went to the Green Derby one night and spent the evening visiting with Fletcher. He stayed until closing time, leaving at the same time Van departed for home. Several hours later, Van was awakened at home by a call from the police. He was told he needed to return to his restaurant at once. When he got there, the player he had been entertaining a few hours earlier was there, too. . . in handcuffs. The police explained they had caught him trying to get Fletcher's safe from the restaurant out to his car.

To be fair, it should be pointed out that very few Gators or former Gators have run into serious trouble with the law, and the Gators have been playing football since 1906. This year's team will be the 95th edition (there was no team in 1943), and the 2006 team will be the 100th.

With the friends he has, Red Mitchum needs no enemies. Jack Nichols, a former teammate, said, "The first game Coach Wolf let Red dress out was for a game in Tampa. Before the kickoff, the alumni had some ceremonies, and part of it was them presenting a bird dog to Coach Wolf. Then just before the kickoff, Coach Wolf called for Red on the sideline. Red thought he was going to be sent in the game, and he grabbed his helmet and ran to Coach Wolf. The coach handed hm the leash for the bird dog and said, 'Hold this dog for me until after the game.' He'd known about the presentation beforehand, and he had brought Red to hold the dog the whole game."

"Red" Mitchum (Photo courtesy of Scott Mitchum)

Nichols also said, "I knew an Auburn player when we were playing, and he told me Red was mentioned in the pregame scouting report. The coaches told the Auburn players, 'Mitchum has deceptive speed. He's a lot slower than he looks.'"

And Nichols again: "Dale Carnegie came to Florida to give a program once. He was famous for his talks about how to act to make everybody like you. He was considered the nicest person in the whole country. Red went to one of the talks and thought it would really help him. Didn't work, though. By the time Red had been in there an hour, Dale Carnegie spit on him."

A former teammate, Cliff Sutton, took Red to Daytona Beach one weekend to see the Atlantic Ocean for the first time. Sutton said, "Red and I stood there on the beach, looking out at the ocean, and Red said, 'It's not as big as I thought it would be.'"

Sutton also said, "We all had money troubles when we were playing for the Gators. Red told me he wished he could make some money by somebody stealing his Plymouth automobile, but I didn't think anything of it. Then some of us went with Red to a bar in a bad neighborhood. I noticed Red left the keys in his car. A couple of hours later I looked out, and two guys were trying to steal the car, but the battery had gone dead. All of a sudden, Red came running up out of the darkness and handed the two guys a jumper cable."

Otis Boggs, who was the Gators' football and basketball play-by-play broadcaster for 40-odd years, provides a story on Chuck Hunsinger, one of the Gators' great runningbacks (1946, '47, '48, '49). Hunsinger was an All-SEC choice in '48 and '49, then played pro football with the Chicago Bears and in the Canadian League. Hunsinger broke the Gators' one-season rushing record (842 yards, '48) and held it for 24 years and broke the career rushing record (2,017 yards) and held it for 17 years. Nat Moore broke Hunsinger's one-season mark with 845 yards in '72, and Larry Smith broke Hunsinger's career rushing record with 2,186 yards, closing his career in 1968.

The present record holders in those departments are Emmitt Smith, one season (1,599 yards, 1989) and Errict Rhett, career (4,163 yards through 1993).

"Hunsinger and a tackle named Frank Dempsey did a lot of hunting together," Boggs said, "and they continued hunting together in later years, going together as teammates to the Chicago Bears

Emmitt Smith had 1,599 rushing yards in 1989 (Photo courtesy of University of Florida Sports Information)

and to the Canadian League. Georgia was our biggest rival in those days. The Bulldogs had beaten us 75-0 in 1942, and then beat us five more games in a row by the time we got to '49, the last season for Hunsinger and Dempsey.

"The week of the Georgia game, I told Chuck, 'If you'll run for over 100 yards and two touchdowns, we'll beat Georgia. If you do that, I'll get you a bird dog as a present.'

"Well, that Saturday in Jacksonville, Hunsinger ran for THREE touchdowns and over 100 yards, and the Gators won, 28-7. I got Chuck a bird dog from Alford Hearin. It was a liver-spotted pointer, and I gave it to Hunsinger and Dempsey. After they'd been out with him a few times, Dempsey told me, 'He's the best dog I've ever seen. He'll run birds down a hole, then put his foot over the hole and let 'em out one at a time for us to shoot at 'em.'"

11

Dock, Blessed Child

One of the most entertaining Gators over the years was Dock Luckie, a defensive tackle from Fort Pierce (1977, '78, '79, '80). He was the biggest and fastest Gator on some of those teams, 6-2, 265 pounds. He set the national high school record in the shot put, the discus and the bench press and was clocked at 9.6 in the 100-yard-dash. A prep All-American in football, he was voted the best high school athlete in the nation. He started for three years for the Gators and played two years in the Canadian Football League, but Dock never lived up to his full promise in football because of a knee problem he suffered when he was hit by a car when he was in the sixth grade. The doctors who treated him were never able to repair the damaged ligament. He had the pain tolerance to play 12 years of football despite the knee, but it reduced his effectiveness. Sometimes it seemed Dock was playing well every other down, and that may have been true, and the pain in his knee often was the cause.

Dock was the butt of many Gator jokes and stories, and that caused some people to suspect he was a clown and not a very smart one. Here are some of the stories associated with Dock. . .

Dock said, "When I was about seven years old, I was walking home from school one day, and a kid ran up behind me and hit me in the back of the head with a steel bar. It left a big hole. You can still see the big scar on my head. People thought I was dead, and they called my mamma. She came running to see about me. The blood was just pouring out. My mother looked to the Heavens and asked God to save me. The wound just closed right up, and I recovered.

"My mama and I both knew after that that I was a blessed child. I've felt that way ever since, and I know I have a responsibility to help people lead better lives, and that's what I do. I was a counselor at the penitentiary at Raiford and talked to 50,000 inmates during my years there. I knew that was the purpose God had for me. I told the inmates that only God could forgive them for their sins. I was able to get my degree and help many people, including friends. I thank God for that. My main duties now with the University Police Department are to educate students about crime on campus. In town and out of town, I speak to athletes and students and sometimes to older people. I'm a motivational speaker, and I enjoy it. Also, I'm a mentor to a lot of athletes.

"One of the stories that they tell on me," Dock said, "is that I picked up a Volkswagen and moved it.

When I first came on campus there was a real big parking problem, and I had to get to class in a hurry. I noticed a Volkswagen in one of the parking spaces. I know now that I did wrong, but the only thing on my mind was to get my car in a parking space and save myself the $5 fee for illegal parking. So I just picked it up and moved it, and I had a parking space then."

In another story about his playing days, Dock dropped by the sports information department during the lunch hour. Most of the employees had gone to lunch, so Dock didn't have any problem sitting down by the Xerox machine and making 60 or 70 copies of his face on the Xerox machine. When the sports information people got back from lunch, they saw what he'd done and were afraid the many Xeroxes might blind Dock. They said his lips were chapped, and his only explanation was that he was trying to take his picture on the Xerox.

Dock laughed when he heard that story and said, "It's true, but what you haven't been told is why I was doing that. We had an 0-10-1 record my junior year, and as we were coming to the end of the school year, I tried to think of what I could do personally to help my team and my teammates. I decided that I could do two things: 1—Give every player a strength-building program for the summer months. 2—Try to loosen everyone up by giving them a few laughs. So I put together this little package for every player on the squad. Each package had my Xerox picture in it and the instructions for the off-season weight program. I also put in little messages to try to loosen them up. We'd been way too tight the year before. A team can't win if it's too tight. A lot of my foolishness was just to loosen them up.

"I can't say I'm the reason for the turnaround, but as you know, my senior season we improved from 0-10-1 to 8-4 with a bowl victory. That's a lot of progress. I think I was successful in getting the players to refocus. My first three years here we didn't have a real strength coach, but players like David Little, David Galloway and myself started the strength program. Under Coach (Doug) Dickey my first two years here, Jack Hall, an assistant coach, did what strength training that we had. I was going well over 500 pounds, and Coach Hall said, 'Dock, you're strong enough. You don't need this. You go to your room and let the weaklings on the team do this.'

"In 1980 when the players came back in the fall, they'd all gone up a lot in their bench press. It made a lot of difference in our team. Some of the guys said to me, 'Let's see if you can really do 500 pounds—blindfolded!' So they blindfolded me, and I didn't know they put 645 pounds for me to do. I did the 645. Then somebody said, 'Let's see how many times you can bench 500 pounds.' They put 500 pounds on for me, and I did it 20 times straight in a row. Nobody ever challenged me to do weights again.'"

Dock remembers Pell's first spring practice with a chuckle: "Cris Collinsworth (three times an All-SEC wide receiver for the Gators) and I overslept and were late for a meeting before the spring game. Our team won the game, and we were all supposed to get a steak, but Cris and I had to eat hot dogs with the losers."

Dock said, "A lot of unusual things happened all during my career. Once I bench-pressed a Toyota. In a high school game, our opponent ran about 60 yards down to our 10-yard-line and fumbled, and I picked up the ball and ran 90 yards for a touchdown. I got more than 200 trophies for track and football. My mama said to me one day, 'You know what you're going to have to do with these trophies, don't you?' I said, 'Yes, ma'm, I'm going to have to give 'em away to the kids in the community.' I gave 'em away as prizes to the kids. I've given all of them away except one—the first trophy I ever won. But I'm going to give that one away, too."

Cris Collinsworth (Photo courtesy of University of Florida Sports Information)

12

A Gator For All Seasons

"The two best things to happen in my life were marrying Grace and attending the University of Florida," Red Mitchum said. "Two of the toughest things I faced in life were when Coach Woodruff came in and put us through 14 weeks of 'spring' practice, and when Coach Woodruff sent me to speak to a booster group at Summerfield, a little town near Ocala. The group had requested a football coach come down and speak to their new organization, but spring practice was going on, and Coach Woodruff asked me to go as a substitute.

"The president got up at the meeting to introduce me and said, 'They said they were going to send us a real football coach, but they didn't do it. They sent this guy. Get up and tell us about football, Hickey.' It was a hard way to start, but they asked me back several times, so I suppose I did all right."

Red moved into a starting offensive tackle job his last two years at UF, but there was at least one occasion when he might have preferred to be back on the bench. That was in 1950 in Lexington when Bear Bryant's Kentucky Wildcats pounded the Gators, 40-6.

"I was playing in front of Bob Gain, Kentucky's All-America tackle, and he was giving me a terrible pounding. This was the Kentucky team that won the SEC championship and beat Oklahoma, the national champion, in the Sugar Bowl.

"The weather was freezing, and we were freezing to death. It was a miserable time. During a timeout, one of our managers came on the field and was wiping the blood off my face. Curtis King came over and looked at me and said, 'Red, you look kinda whupped.' I just shook my head, and Curtis said, 'We're getting whupped bad, but you know what we oughta do? When we come out of the huddle for the next play, we need to holler something, even if we have to take it back!'"

"When I was first at Florida, I wasn't getting to do much," Mitchum said. "At practice I was a 'stander.' I just stood off to the side with some other players who weren't much good, either. One day Hunsinger was running the ball, and as he ran past us he hit me with a shoulder and kept running down the field. He was just

Art Pepin, Jimmy Kynes, Stan Musial, and Red Mitchum at the Governor's Baseball Dinner. (Photo courtesy of Scott Mitchum)

playing with me. As he ran back past us, I hit him with a shoulder. Coach Wolf just saw the part where I hit Hunsinger, and he yelled, 'Mitchum, don't bother the football players!'"

At a roast honoring Mitchum at a Golden Era reunion at Crystal River in July of 2000, the chairman of the roast committee was Marvene Hawkins, wife of ex-Gator Joe Hawkins. As she began introducing the guest of honor, she said, "Once in a lifetime, if you're lucky, a genuinely funny man comes along to be a part of your group. Until he gets here, we'll just have to get by with Red."

Jack Nichols' salute to Red that night included this: "Red always says the two luckiest things to happen to him were coming to the University of Florida and finding a woman who was smart, kind, charming and all the things that would make you want to keep her the rest of your life. Red, I remember how scared you used to be that Grace was going to find out about her."

I'll leave it up to you to figure out which of the things said about Red were true and which weren't, but I can vow that Red and Grace have been one of the great married couples I've ever known . . . totally devoted to each other. However, when Grace was given a chance at the roast to put in her two cents worth on Red, she said, "I'll have to say Red is solely responsible for what I am today . . . depressed."

Red tells a story about a hard-working family that lived near his family in Gadsden, Alabama. The husband and wife and five kids lived in a one-room house. The husband came home one day with a goat. His wife said, "What in the world are you going to do with that goat?" The husband replied, "This goat is going to make us a lot of money." The wife said, "You and your great ideas. I bet you haven't even figured out where we're going to keep that goat."

The husband said, "This is a valuable goat. We're going to let him live in the house with the rest of us." The wife made a terrible frown and said, "The smell is really going to be awful!" Said the husband, "That's all right. The goat is just going to have to get used to the smell!"

Red and Marcelino Huerta were great friends until Huerta's death, but they constantly insulted each other. I remember once when each one took a shot at the other, attaching an insult to something he thought his cohort might be touchy about. Huerta thought Red was probably thin-skinned about the question of whether he was really a first-team player or not, and Red thought Huerta might be self-conscious about his large head.

"Red was a terrible player," Huerta said. "Somebody told me Red had newspaper clippings that showed he was a first-team player for the Gators. I was there when Red was trying to play football. He was awful! There's a place in the French Quarter in New Orleans that will print you a fake newspaper saying anything you want it to say. You can get a newspaper with a headline, 'Mitchum Awarded Congressional Medal of Honor.' Or 'Marilyn Monroe Admits Her Love for Red Mitchum.' Or, worst of all, 'Mitchum Leads Gators Against Tulane.' That had to be where he got those line-ups that show him starting."

Mitchum got his turn and said, "Chelo went to Africa once and got captured by some pygmy head hunters. But they turned him loose when they found out there was no way they could shrink his head."

13

Gator Clan McGriff

Lee McGriff is a member of one of the most illustrious families in Gator sports history. His father, Jack, lettered in track at UF and was football head coach at the university's laboratory school, P.K. Yonge. Cousin Perry lettered two years in football at UF ('58-59) and was an All-America in baseball. Lee began as a walk-on but lettered three years in football ('72, '73 and '74), twice led the SEC in pass receiving and was first-team All-SEC.

Perry's son, Mark, lettered three years ('86, '87 and '88) and was a starter at tight end. Lee's son, Travis, lettered four years at wide receiver ('95, '96, '97 and '98), broke the SEC record for most pass reception yards in a single season and was first team All-SEC and third-team AP All-America. Lee also coached the Gator wide receivers for five years before retiring to enter business in Gainesville.

Lee offers these stories: "I'll never forget when we went to Auburn to play in '73. We'd lost four straight games, we had never beaten Auburn at Cliff Hare Stadium and Coach Dickey was making a very sensitive change at quarterback (from junior David Bowden to sophomore Don Gaffney). There was a lotta tension on that whole trip. Coach Dickey always called on a senior at the pregame meal to say thanks. But this time, with everybody uptight, he called on sophomore fullback Jimmy DuBose, who was real shy.

"Everybody bowed their heads, and it seemed like five minutes before DuBose said a word. Finally he said, 'Dear Lord,' and his voice cracked. Then he said, 'Thanks for bringing me back to Auburn, Alabama.' Well, we all knew Jimmy had never been to Auburn before in his life. He rambled through a lot of nothing.

"We went out that day and beat Auburn for the first time in that stadium, 12-8, and we called Jimmy 'Rev. DuBose' after that. Dickey had never done anything like that before, calling on a sophomore to say thanks, but for the rest of my career I always kept a blessing in my pocket in case I suddenly got called on."

"One of the funniest things was the night before the Florida-Georgia game in '73 in Jacksonville. Our team always went to a movie on Friday night, and our bus pulled up to the movie theatre at the exact same time as Georgia's team bus. The teams had picked the same movie. The two head coaches, Coach Dickey and Vince Dooley, got out and started talking, and they went on and on. It was obvious the coaches didn't want all those players in the same theatre, but neither one wanted to give the appearance that he was giving in to the other team. It looked like they were going to be talking all night. Finally it was agreed that BOTH teams would go into the theatre. We were on one side, and Georgia was on the other. Nothing happened, but you could have cut the tension in that theatre with a butter knife."

Lee was too modest to make mention of the fact that the next day he made a late, diving catch in the end zone of a Don Gaffney pass for a touchdown, and Gaffney threw to tight end Hank Foldberg for a two-point conversion, and Florida won, 11-10. . .

"Jimbo Kynes (Gator center) was my roommate and was very special to me," Lee said. "Like his brother, Bill, he was a serious student. Not all our players were as academic as Jimbo. Jimbo would get on anyone who was not going to class. One night, someone rattled our door in the dorm. Jimbo said, 'I think they're doing something to our door.' I said I didn't care, I was going to sleep.

"Then they put a crutch across the door, which would lock you in your room. We could tell that's what they did, and Jimbo said, 'If we don't do something, we can't go to class.' I was just trying to go to sleep and didn't much care, but Jimbo was so upset he threw his weight against the door, and that snapped the crutch, and it made a tremendous noise. Everybody came running out of the other rooms to see what the explosion was."

And Lee told this most unusual story about himself, the Gator wide receiver coach, and Charley Pell, the new Gator head coach, who came in in December, 1978, and Lee swears every word is true:

"Coach Pell had been there about two weeks. Doug Knotts, the outgoing defensive coordinator, sat me down and said, 'I don't know whether you want to coach with this guy.' He was real down on Pell, which was natural for a guy not being kept by the new coach. From Pell's first day, it was a 24-hour job coaching the Gators, and he wanted the assistants to feel the same way.

"I was going to scout a high school playoff game in Miami. I got a flight and took just enough money to get through one night in Miami and fly back to Gainesville. After the game I went to my hotel room and went to sleep and about 2 a.m. I got this call from Pell. He called all of us 'Coach.' 'Coach, what are you doing for the Gators?' I thought, 'I'm trying to get some sleep,' but I didn't think I should tell him that. I couldn't get an answer out. He told me he wanted me to stay the next two days recruiting in Miami and Fort Myers. I told him about my lack of money and that I had been expecting to return to Gainesville Saturday.

"He went silent. Then he told me, 'Coach, you've got this problem. Call me when you have a serious problem.' And he hung up.

"I phoned Margie (Lee's wife) and told her to meet me at the Gainesville airport the next morning when my plane got in. This was the old Gainesville airport. I told her to park over behind another building and to stay out of sight. I thought he might be in the terminal. When I got off the plane the next morning, I crouched down and almost crawled from the plane. I jumped over a fence and ran to my car and lay down on the floor. Really. After I dropped Margie off, I drove to Fort Myers, where he'd told me to go. All of us who stayed together all these years will tell you it was sometimes hard to deal with Coach Pell."

Lee stayed on Pell's staff four years before deciding to go into business in Gainesville.

14

The Birth of Gatorade

Eddie Foster, a Gator defensive tackle in '68, has several memories of his playing days:

"We were playing LSU at Florida Field in '65. They ran all over us, but they had trouble getting the ball into the end zone, and somehow we won, 14-7. Steve Spurrier was our quarterback. Dr. Robert Cade was experimenting with us for his Gatorade invention, which proved to be a great drink, but it wasn't always good when he first started working with it. Allen Trammell, who was a defensive back, had had too much Gatorade, and he wasn't feeling very well, but he went in to run a punt back. As he was waiting under the punt, he started throwing up . . . bigtime. But he was able to concentrate and make the catch at the same time, and he made about a 25-yard return. LSU had a defensive end named Carl Granger, who was right on top of Trammell when he caught the ball, but Granger sort of veered away and let Trammell past him. The LSU coaches were giving Granger hell on the sideline, and some of our players heard Granger, in his Cajun accent, say, 'Mon, I no could tackle him. Mon, he was puking! . . .'"

"The next year we played LSU over in Baton Rouge, and we won what was a blowout back then, 28-7. Granger got in trouble again, this time for holding Don Giordano, a defensive tackle for us. Granger shouted, 'Mon, I not holding that mon!' Giordano, who was from New York before he moved to Miami, said, 'What kind of talk is that?' We all thought Giordano talked funny, but Cajun seemed like crazy talk to Gio. . . ."

"The early part of football practice each year, one day we all had to run a mile over at the track, timed by our trainer, Brady Greathouse. The linemen had to run it in six minutes, the backs in five-and-a-half minutes, etc. This was to let the coaches know if we'd been working out during the summer. Well, Brady would set himself up at one place on the track and would sit down with the watch and time everybody from there. He would call off the minutes while the players were running.

"Some of the linemen had trouble making the times they'd been assigned, and Giordano was one of them. Down at the opposite end of the field from where Brady was sitting, there were some tables used by the scorers and timers in track. They were piled up, and on his first trip around, Giordano peeled off and lay down behind those tables. Everybody could see Gio was getting away with it, so a whole bunch of us sat down behind the tables the next time around. Then on the last lap we all came out from behind the tables and sprinted to the finish line. Brady got excited and said, 'Man, this is the best shape a Florida team has ever been in! Some of you linemen ran a 4:50! I can't believe it!'

"We went on back to the dressing room, knowing we had put something over on the coaches, but the coaches got somebody to squeal on us—I don't know who it was—and we had to run it over the next day."

"The football team moved into Yon Hall (the new football dormitory) in '67. I was rooming with Jim Yarbough (tight end), and we were right next door to Guy Dennis (offensive guard) and George Dean (defensive end). A lot of us did some hunting, and one night I loaned my shotgun to Dean. He asked me how he should clean it, and I told him there were two ways, one of which included pulling the trigger. Dean pulled the trigger, and there was a cartridge in the gun, and it blew a hole in the ceiling in our room.

"Brand new freshmen were staying in the room above ours, and we went running up there to see if they were all right. I said a prayer on the way up that we wouldn't find them gathered around one of the freshmen players.

"We got up there, and the freshmen were all running around asking what happened. They said, 'Somebody was shooting at us,' and of course that was true. But the shot hadn't gotten through their floor. We managed to keep it hushed up, and Dean tried to plug up the hole in the ceiling, using everything from chewing gum on up. If anybody ever noticed the hole, it was years later after we'd graduated, and they didn't know which class was guilty. Nobody ever said anything about it."

15

Man of Few Words

Warren Fair, a Gator letterman at guard in '57, furnished several stories for the book. I was put onto him by halfback Bill Newbern, who now lives in Huntsville, Alabama, but who was a classmate of Fair's at Jacksonville Landon High and then a roommate at UF.

One of the favorite subjects of Fair, who now lives in Gainesville, was his Gator coach, Bob Woodruff. He described Woodruff as well as I think anyone could:

"He was a very intelligent person who came out with some of the damnedest things. In the '53 Rice game in Houston, the lights went out with five minutes left in the half, with the Gators leading by 10 points. For the 25 minutes that the lights were out, Woodruff sat on the coaches' bench and didn't say a word. Just a few minutes before the lights came back on, Woodruff turned to Hobe Hooser (defensive line coach), who'd been sitting next to him the whole time and said, 'Somebody turned the lights out.' When the lights came back on, halfback Dicky Moegle of Rice started running wild, and they beat us, 20-16."

In the Cotton Bowl at the end of the season, Rice thumped Alabama, and the winners were awarded one of their touchdowns when Tommy Lewis of Alabama came off the bench to tackle Moegle, who was in the clear and apparently headed for a touchdown.

"Someone described Coach Woodruff as the oratorical equivalent of a blocked punt," Fair said. That Woodruff was capable of poking fun at himself was proved when he took that description and applied it to himself often in his talks.

"A lot of people swear he made the same pep talk every game, and he did," Fair said. "Just a few words were different sometimes. I still remember his talks, especially one time when he said, 'Get out there and tackle 'em HARD and block 'em HARD, and don't forget, the team that makes the fewest mistakes always makes the fewest mistakes. . . .'"

"We were studying film on Wednesday night before the game one week. It was pitch black dark in there, and Coach Woodruff kept running the film backward and forward. Then we all noticed a strange smell in the room. Woodruff smoked cigarettes at the time, and this deep voice of his came out of the dark, 'Lit the wrong end. . . .'"

"When we were scrimmaging, Coach Woodruff constantly would say, 'Run that play back.' One day the players prepared for him to say that after a pitchout from the quarterback to the halfback, and when he said it, the players ran the play backwards, like it would be re-run when you backed the film up. Every player ran backward from downfield back to the huddle. They even had it arranged where the running back pitched the ball forward to the quarterback, and the quarterback ran backwards to his spot under center. It broke everybody up, including the coaches."

Fair said Woodruff may have been his funniest after the Florida-Georgia game of '58. Georgia had about 400 yards of offense to Florida's 100, but Georgia fouled up consistently in scoring territory, and the Gators won the game, 7-6, on a 78-yard run by quarterback Jimmy Dunn.

"Georgia was already mad about the game," Fair said, "and when it was over, Coach Woodruff walked up to shake hands with Wally Butts, Georgia's coach, and said, 'How did you like our offense, Wally?'"

Fists were thrown at some postgame parties because of comments like that, but Butts was able to restrain himself regarding Woodruff's comment. Dick Stratton, Jacksonville TV sports director and a UF graduate, showed up at the Green Derby restaurant in Jacksonville with the game's official statistics about an hour after the game. One of Georgia's assistant coaches was in the room as Stratton read the stats in dramatic fashion, something like this: "First downs, Georgia 18, Florida 4. Rushing yards, Georgia 280, Florida 90.

Passing yards, Georgia 120, Florida 10. Total yards, Georgia 400, Florida 100. But the most important statistic of all: Points, Georgia 6, Florida 7."

The Florida fans in the crowd broke into applause, but the Georgia assistant coach jumped up and decked Stratton with a right to the jaw. There's disagreement about who the Georgia assistant was, so his identity is being withheld.

Woodruff salutes Mitchum. (Photo courtesy of Scott Mitchum)

16

The Gator Flop

Perhaps the most famous play in Gator history was the Gator Flop against Miami in 1971. I never saw anything like what happened in the final minutes of the Gators' 45-16 triumph over the Miami Hurricanes in Orange Bowl Stadium. I was a witness, but everyone who was there seems to remember the play a little bit differently, including different versions by the Gator players who were involved.

This was the situation: The Gators had sloughed through a 3-7 season up to the Miami game. John Reaves, Carlos Alvarez, Tommy Durrance and other members of the sophomore class in the spectacular 1969 season (9-1-1, including a Gator Bowl victory over SEC champion Tennessee) weren't happy seniors in '71. The beatings had been severe, and several players were still disgruntled that Tennessee Coach Doug Dickey had

*John Reaves (Photo courtesy of University of Florida
Sports Information)*

succeeded Ray Graves as Gator coach after the '69 Gator Bowl meeting. Miami was a slight favorite going into the '71 game in its first season under former Miami quarterback Fran Curci, an avowed Gator hater.

Reaves, going into the final game of his college career, was within 344 yards of the national career passing record held by Jim Plunkett of Stanford (7,545 yards). That seemed to be a nearly impossible reach for Reaves, who had averaged 290 passing yards per game in '69, 232 yards in '70 and was averaging 176 yards going into the Miami game. Reaves had surpassed 344 yards just twice in his career: 369 yards against Auburn and 346 yards against Miami, both in his sophomore season.

The two leading characters in this drama were to be Curci and Reaves, who didn't like each other. The year before when he was head coach at the University of Tampa, Curci had described the Reaves-led Gators as crybabies. Reaves had expressed his displeasure about Curci. Now they were opponents as Reaves took aim at one of the game's top records.

Reaves was hotter against Miami than he'd been in any game in two years. Late in the fourth quarter the Gators, amazingly, had a 39-9 lead, and Reaves, also amazingly, had thrown for 331 yards and was within 13 yards of the record. Curci's Miami team appeared to be running out the clock with a tedious series of running plays. The Gators got Miami stopped and forced a punt, but Gator cornerback Harvin Clark ran the punt back for a touchdown, and Miami got the ball again. More running plays. Clark apologized to Reaves for his touchdown, for depriving him of a chance at the record. Twice Clark called timeout and asked Dickey to allow Miami to score, because it was going to be the only chance Reaves would get one last shot at the record. Twice Dickey refused. With 1:20 left in the game and Miami at the Gator 7-yard line, third down coming up, the Gators used their final timeout. People in the press box and in the UM radio booth predicted the Gators would intentionally let Miami score. Clark begged Dickey a third time, and this time Dickey said, "OK, but don't make it look bad."

Clark ran to the defensive huddle. I asked John Clifford, the Gators' junior free safety, to finish the story of what happened. Clifford was from Coral Gables, home of the University of Miami, and has coached high school football for many years at P.K. Yonge, UF's laboratory school in Gainesville. I have heard several stories that Clifford was the only Gator that night who declined to flop.

"Harvin came into the huddle," Clifford said, "and told us, 'Coach says to let 'em score! We're all going to lie down!' I didn't flop, but I've been told that I stood up on the play, and that isn't so. I went down to one knee and didn't make a move to make the tackle.

"I've looked at some pictures of the play, and one of our players WAS standing up, but it wasn't me. I don't know who it was. I've been told I tried to make the tackle, but I didn't do that either. What I remember best is the look on (Miami quarterback) John Hornibrook's face when he rolled out and saw all those people on the ground. He hesitated a moment, and

*Carlos Alvarez (Photo courtesy of University of Florida
Sports Information)*

maybe his instincts took over, and he kind of walked across the goal. I've often wondered how weird it would have gotten if he had declined to score the TD and had run back up the field with the ball. That play might have gone on a long time.

"After the touchdown, we got the ball back, and John hit Carlos for 15 yards to break the record." The coaches had Reaves throw one more pass in case the addition wasn't right, and he hit Hollis Boardman for two yards.

"The coaches turned John loose a little more than usual in that game," Clifford said. "Let him throw more. But I'll always believe we could have done it better on the laydown play . . . done it without embarrassing anyone. But I never considered myself any better than anybody else because I didn't flop. There was a lot of frustration on that team. We'd had a lousy season, and we weren't going to a bowl game. The frustration of the whole season came out that night. Also, I remember a lot of enthusiasm among the players before the game about John having a shot at the record.

"When the game was over, I don't know who started it, but we all ran down behind the end zone where the pool was for the Miami Dolphins' mascot, Flipper. We all jumped in the water and just splashed around, whooping it up."

I believe the two strangest scenes ever for me in more than 60 years of watching football were the laydown play and the players diving in Flipper's pool, and they came within about three minutes of each other.

Curci has devoted a lot of his life since that night to criticizing the Gator Flop. He had much to say about it from that night on. For years I thought Curci just saw an opportunity to get the spotlight off him and his team's poor performance. Miami was favored in the game and lost by a 45-16 score, and Curci installed a new offense the week of the game (the wishbone) and moved Miami's great running back, Chuck Foreman, later a longtime NFL star with the Minnesota Vikings, to flanker, where he didn't carry the ball a single time.

My thought was Curci was standing on the sideline with about a minute to play, thinking how he was going to be criticized, when the laydown play presented itself . . . and presented Curci with a substitute scapegoat for everyone to focus on. People who have coached with Curci tell me, "No, he was really bitter about the laydown play, and many years later he was still cussing Dickey and blaming him for it."

OK, I'll concede that Curci was truly hacked, but I never thought Dickey deserved any criticism for the play. Most coaches I believe would have let the opposition score, and the flop was the last thing Dickey wanted to happen.

17

Youngblood's Panty Raid

Jack Youngblood may have been the greatest defensive player in Gator history. For sure, he's the only Gator in the Pro Football Hall of Fame at the moment, having been elected in January, 2001. Youngblood, who played at little Monticello High near Tallahassee, was 16 years old his senior season and weighed 180 pounds. The Gators took a chance on him . . . and won.

Youngblood grew into a 6-foot-4, 235-pound defensive end by his junior year and was perhaps the best defensive player on the outstanding '69 team. In '70 he was an All-America choice, and he had a long and successful career with the Los Angeles Rams. Perhaps the game he's most famous for was a losing experience in the Super Bowl against the Pittsburgh Steelers. Youngblood had a broken leg and played every defensive down. The Rams led until the fourth quarter, then lost to one of the great machines in NFL history.

Asked for his funniest memory with the Gators, Youngblood chose a panty raid his freshman year.

"It wasn't really a panty raid," Youngblood said. "We just wanted to harass some girls. But we got arrested, and the campus cops took us to the university police station. I was allowed one call, and I knew I had to call my freshman coach, Jimmy Haynes, to come get us out. Jimmy was a tough little guy. I would rather they call my mother than call him. It turned out to be a blessing in disguise. Haynes made me get up and run every morning for the next month. When he got through with me, I was in the best shape of my life, and after that I was a lot better football player. I may not have done the things I later did if Coach Haynes hadn't worked me so much after the raid."

William "Bubba" McGowan was a Gator letterman halfback in '50 and '51 and coached the Gator wide receivers from '65 through '69, his best players including Casey, Trapp and Alvarez. He's coached the last 25 years at Buchholz High in Gainesville.

"My favorite recruiting story was in December, 1966," McGowan said, "and it was about Donnie Williams. Donnie was a heckuva linebacker at Lake City Columbia High, and he was highly recruited. The day before signing day, Coach Graves phoned from out of town and told me somebody in Lake City had called him and said Bear Bryant (Alabama football coach) was coming to Williams' house that night to try to recruit him. He said, 'Get up there and get with Eldridge Beach at the highway patrol station, and y'all try to save this kid for us.' Eldridge, an ex-Gator football player, was a colonel in the Florida Highway Patrol and was the head of it for many years. I drove to Lake City, and there Eldridge was waiting for me. He already had directions to Donnie's house.

"We drove there and talked to Donnie a while, and Eldridge said, 'Let's go for a ride.' We got Donnie in the Highway Patrol car and took off. We weren't going to bring him back until the next day. After a few hours Eldridge called back and talked to Donnie's mama. She said, 'Bear Bryant's been sitting in our living room for almost two hours, waiting on Donnie to come home.' Eldridge said, 'Tell him Donnie had to go off on some kinda business and won't be back until tomorrow.' We kept Donnie with us the next day until we had him signed." (Recruiting rules in those days weren't as strict as they are now.)

"In the summer all the assistant coaches used to work at Ray Graves Summer Camps all over the state," McGowan said. "In '67 we were down at the camp in Fort Lauderdale, and Gene Ellenson (defensive coordinator) was in charge because Graves had to go somewhere else. We'd hired the top two players in the Heisman Trophy race in '66 to help us with the camp, Spurrier from Florida and Bob Griese from Purdue. Griese was a rookie with the Miami Dolphins. "Well, Graves hired Spurrier for $500, and then he had to pay Griese $1,000 to get him. Spurrier found out Griese was getting $1,000, and he really complained to Ellenson, and Gene had to raise him to $1,000, too. 'I've been in charge one day,' Ellenson said, 'and I've already lost $500 for Graves.' That problem didn't come up again because the next year Griese started his own camp, ran it just like we ran ours and made a lot of money out of it. We didn't have Griese any more."

Steve Spurrier (Photo courtesy of University of Florida Sports Information)

18

Casares' Last Fight

Rick Casares was one of the University of Florida's greatest all-around athletes, indeed, one of the finest all-around athletes any school ever had. He was the New Jersey state heavyweight Golden Gloves champion at the age of 15 (no one under 16 was supposed to be admitted to the competition). He completed high school at Tampa. At the University of Florida, standing 6-2 and weighing 210 pounds, he was second-team All-SEC fullback his junior year after starting the early games that year at quarterback. He was drafted into the service during his senior campaign and never had the chance to fully show what he was capable of doing in college football.

He was also the Gators' best basketball player, and his junior year he helped Florida win the Gator Bowl football game on Saturday (the Gators' first bowl appearance ever), then joined the Gator basketball team on Monday night, without any practice at all, for the two-night Gator Bowl tournament and won the tournament's Most Valuable Player award. With the Chicago Bears, his weight up to 225 pounds, he was All-National Football League fullback in '56, led the league in rushing and played a large role in getting the Bears to the NFL championship game, where they were defeated by the New York Giants.

Jim Brown, considered by many to be the best running back in NFL history, came into the league in '57 with the Cleveland Browns, and for several years Brown and Casares were one-two each season, in that order, in the competition for top NFL fullback.

Casares was a legend before he departed UF. In the dormitory, Norm Carlson and Curt Cunkle roomed next to Casares. Carlson had come to UF on a basketball scholarship and was later sports information director and for many years assistant athletic director. Cunkle was a burly basketball player (and a good one), built very similar to Casares.

John Mauer, Gator basketball coach, remembered his days with Casares and Cunkle fondly. "We were as tough as anybody on the boards," Mauer said. "Rick and Curt weren't but 6-2, and there were some players in the SEC 10 inches taller, but we still won a lot of rebounding battles. Most of the time the opposition would go high and get first possession of the rebound, but on the way back down, Casares or Cunkle would take it away from them or at least get a jump ball."

Carlson vividly remembers the Casares-Cunkle days at UF: "Rick would decide he wanted to go to Jacksonville to have some fun, and he'd make Cunkle go with him. A lot of people at UF were scared of Cunkle, but Cunkle was afraid to cross Rick . . . with good reason. One night Curt was studying for a test and said he couldn't go with Rick, and Rick went to his room and got a shotgun. Cunkle locked the door to our room, and he and I were standing a little bit away from the door, off to the side, and a shotgun blast came right through the door. Cunkle decided right then that he DID want to go to Jacksonville. When they got back, Rick said they'd had a real good time."

Rick's teammates furnished this story about a Gator basketball game against Ole Miss at Oxford. Things got pretty rough, and an Ole Miss player came up on the blind side and hit Casares in the nose with a round-house right. Blood spewed from Rick's nose. The officials put the Ole Miss player out of the game. Casares sat on the Florida bench, with a towel pressed against his nose. The ejected player sat on the Ole Miss bench, and Casares glared at him. A few minutes later, the Ole Miss player left the bench and went down a winding staircase that led to both teams' dressing quarters. Casares dropped the towel and ran to the staircase and started down. Coaches and players on both teams sensed what was about to happen and started down the stairs also.

They got within viewing distance and saw what happened at the bottom of the stairs. The Ole Miss player had picked up a steel chair and bashed Casares over the head with it. Some more blood squirted out of Casares, but Rick took advantage of the small amount of time he had before the posse could reach him. He landed two tremendous punches to the jaw of the Ole Miss player, knocking him unconscious. Both players were taken to the hospital, in separate vehicles, which was wise. Casares had to get several stitches in his scalp, but the Ole Miss player had to be treated for two fractures of the jaw.

Basketball games in Oxford, Mississippi, were played in relative privacy at that time, and no report of the fight appeared at the time in newspapers. But several Casares teammates confirmed the unpleasantness that happened.

Casares the soldier was stationed at Fort Jackson, S.C., where he was a member of the post's football and basketball teams. This was just after the Korean War, so there was no great haste on the part of Fort Jackson officials for Casares to complete basic training.

Basic required 13 weeks of training, but every time Casares was on the verge of completing it, he would go on a long trip with the football or basketball team, and when he returned he was forced to restart basic training. This went on for months and months, which wasn't pleasing to Rick, since the soldiers in basic training had to rise at 5:30 a.m.

Rick finally wearied of basic and went to see the battalion commander, a colonel, to see if he could get some relief. The colonel listened to the complaint as he studied Rick's personnel papers. When Rick was through talking, the colonel said, "I see on your personal record that you won the New Jersey Golden Gloves when you were 15 years old. Well, we have a post heavyweight champion who is the most overbearing, obnoxious soldier on the base. He thinks he's going to be the next heavyweight champion of the world. Well, I would do a lot to see somebody beat this guy. I'll make a deal with you. I'll set up a fight between you and him, and if you beat him, I'll give you credit for completing basic training."

"That sounded like a fair deal to me," Casares said. "So the colonel got two pairs of boxing gloves and had his jeep driver take both of us down to the area where the post heavyweight champion stayed. The colonel got all the soldiers in that unit to form a huge ring around us, and we were going to fight right there in the company area. He told the post champion that I was challenging him for the post championship, and the champion kinda shrugged like, 'OK, if he wants to, it's fine with me.' You could tell he wasn't worried. So that's where we fought."

And Casares immediately turned his attention to other matters, like that was that for his story. Others in the conversation asked him for the result of the fight. How did it end?

"Like I said," Casares said, "the colonel said I had to win to get credit for having completed basic train-

ing. So this fight was real important to me. We fought
for a while, and then an Army ambulance crew came
down to the area and picked up the champion and put
him in the back of it and took him to the post hospital.
I didn't have anything against the guy, but I HAD to
get out of basic training."

The first time I met Rick Casares, I asked him
something about George Halas, the Chicago Bears'
longtime owner and coach. "You've just ruined a nice
evening by bringing up that guy's name," Casares said.
I asked him what was so bad about Halas, and Rick
replied: "He was a terrible person to play for. He had
no sympathy for his players. He hired a private detective to follow me on my off hours one season."

A year or so later, Halas had brought his Bears to
Jacksonville to play an exhibition game. We had dinner together, and I told him that Casares had told me
that Halas had a private detective follow him.

"Yes, I did," said Halas, "and I'll tell you what happened. Rick was single, and I suspected that he was
doing too much socializing with the ladies. The detective followed him for several weeks and reported back
to me that three different women were going over to
Rick's apartment EVERY DAY. One would come in
about 7 a.m. before he reported to the Bears. Another
would come in about 6 p.m. after he got home. Then
another would come in after dinner, like 9 p.m. I called
Rick in and told him what I'd found out about his activities. I said, 'Rick, you're considered the second best

fullback in the NFL behind Jim Brown. If you would cut down on these activities to just one a day, you might be the No. 1 fullback in the NFL.' He thought for just a moment, then said, 'Coach, I think I'll just keep on with what I'm doing and be No. 2.'"

The night before one exhibition game in Jacksonville involving the Chicago Bears, the UF alumni had a big party at one of the hotels. The ole grads were particularly pleased when one of the greatest ex-Gators, Rick Casares, dropped in for a visit of an hour or so. He was accompanied by Bill George, the Bears' All-NFL middle linebacker. Casares was a big focal point of the night for the alumni. The next day I ran into Halas before the game, and we chatted briefly. I mentioned that the Gator alumni appreciated Halas letting Casares come to the party the night before.

"Was Bill George there?" Halas asked. I replied in the affirmative and said, "I was surprised to see a Wake Forest alumnus at the Gator party. I wonder why he was there."

"I asked him to go," Halas said. "I wanted Casares to leave the party early and come back to our hotel, and George is the toughest guy on the team. I felt George reminding Rick about our curfew might have some influence on him. Rick wouldn't pay attention to anybody else but George."

19

D'Agostino's Rattlesnake

Two of the sharpest Gators in '50, '51 and '52 were Maurice Edmonds and Hill Brannon. They were the student-managers, and they were accepted as companions and equals by the players. Edmonds made the Army his career, retired as a major general and now lives in Ponte Vedra on the Atlantic Ocean near Jacksonville.

L to R: Hill Brannon, Jr. (Mgr.), William Kerkesner (Equip. Mgr.), Maurice Edmonds (Mgr.) (Photo courtesy of Hill Brannon, Jr.)

Brannon had a suc-
cessful career in business
and now lives in retire-
ment in Keystone
Heights, close enough to
Gainesville to allow him
to follow Gator football
closely.

They tell some inter-
esting stories about their
days at UF when Casares
and defensive guard Joe
D'Agostino were their
next-door roommates.
The first Gator interior
linemen to win All-SEC
honors were Jimmy

Charlie LaPradd (Photo
courtesy of University of
Florida Sports Information)

Kynes (center) in '49 and Charlie LaPradd (tackle) and
D'Agostino, both in '52. LaPradd was the Gators' first
All-America interior lineman, and Ralph Cellon introduced him as such at a civic club breakfast in Gainesville
years later, adding that LaPradd got the honor "only
because the All-America committee called Woodruff
and asked him the name of his great lineman, and Woodruff knew he'd never be able to spell D'Agostino."

"Joe-Joe D'Agostino roomed with Rick Casares,"
Edmonds said, "and he knew Rick was deathly afraid
of snakes. Joe-Joe took a dead rattlesnake and wrapped
it up in Rick's newspaper and laid it on Rick's bed. Rick
jumped so high he hit his head on the ceiling and almost knocked himself out. He paid Joe-Joe back by

putting Joe's textbooks side by side and taking a rifle and firing a bullet that went right through the center of all of them."

"Rick was on the second floor of Murphree Hall," Brannon said, "and he saw Cunkle walking toward the dorm. There was a dempsey-dumpster right by where Cunkle was walking, and Rick shot his rifle at the dempsey dumpster and almost scared Cunkle to death. Everybody in those days had a shotgun or a rifle. One day Buford Long and Sammy Oosterhoudt had their guns out, and they were chasing me. I jumped in the dempsey dumpster, and they fired four or five shots off the dumpster. We did some crazy things in those days."

"There was a basketball game one year between the football players and the basketball players," Brannon said. "Everybody was drinking beer after the game, and we wound up out at Stengle Field, a private airport on the edge of town. Several football players climbed up and sat on an airplane and crushed the fuselage. The man that owned the plane went to Woodruff about it, and the man said he wouldn't press charges if we paid him $300 to repair the plane.

"We all put in $3 or $5, but two players said they weren't going to pay because they didn't drink and didn't have anything to do with the damage to the plane. They were J. Pappa Hall (halfback) and Mack Gilstrap (linebacker). The next morning Mitchum knocked on their door at 5 a.m. Red said he was going to give them a similar wake-up call every morning until they kicked in their share. That day wasn't over before they'd paid up. It wasn't worth the money to get that early wake-up call every morning."

"The football team was flying to Nashville in '50 to play Vanderbilt," Edmonds said. "On the plane Mitchum kept sending water back to Curtis King. He told him that drinking a lot of water would eliminate air sickness. Just as Red had planned, eventually Curtis had to get up and go to the restroom. When he did, Red got up and got on the plane's intercom system and imitated Curtis' voice. It was the first time he'd imitated Curtis in front of the squad. Red (a.k.a. Curtis) announced on the intercom, 'Don't want to upset nobody, but the right wing has fallen off this plane.' It was the first plane trip for a lot of the players, and a lot of the players and some of the coaches jumped up in fright and looked out the window. Red slipped back into his seat, and just then Curtis left the restroom and started walking down the aisle. He hadn't heard any of the commotion.

"Coach Woodruff saw Curtis and growled, 'Curtis, you need to get your mind on the game!' Then Coach (Frank) Broyles (then a Gator assistant) saw Curtis and growled, 'Curtis, you ought to get your mind on the game!' Coach John Sauer (also an assistant) had been particularly frightened by the missing wing announcement, and he jumped up and got Curtis by the shoulder and sat him down forcefully in his seat and told him, 'You BETTER get your mind on the game, King!'

"Curtis shook his head and said quietly to the player sitting next to him, 'Gollee! These people want you to keep your mind on the game even when you're taking a leak.'"

Mitchum's humor didn't hurt the team. Vandy was a heavy favorite, but the next day the Gators scored their first important victory of Woodruff's reign, a 31-27 triumph over the Commodores.

Brannon and LaPradd are great friends, but Brannon still shakes his head about some criticism he got years ago. "You asked me back in the early '80s about LaPradd's playing days," Brannon said. "I told you about the time Bobby Flowers blocked a punt at Auburn, and LaPradd picked it up and 'lumbered' into the end zone. First, LaPradd got on me about my choice of words that ran in your column, but what was worse, his wife got on me about it. 'Charlie didn't LUMBER over the goal,' she said. 'He RAN over!' I asked Hobe Hooser, who had been the Gators' defensive line coach at that time, and Hobe said, 'I think lumber is probably the best word to describe what he did.'

"Hooser was one of the best-loved coaches Florida ever had. He coached a long time at Lake City High, and he had a lot of friends all over the state. When he was at the University of Arkansas, he got Pat Summerall of Lake City to go to Arkansas, and LaPradd, who was from St. Augustine, went with a buddy of his to Arkansas to try out (which was legal at that time). Hobe talked to the two boys after the tryout, and he told Charlie's buddy he would get him a scholarship at an Arkansas small college, and he told Charlie that he didn't think he could play college football.

"A few years later Hobe was hired as Florida's line coach, and he was introduced to his tackles, who included LaPradd, who'd grown a lot by then. Hobe told Charlie, 'I've known you somewhere, but I just can't come up with it.' Charlie smiled and said, 'You told me at Arkansas that I couldn't play college football, but now I'm ALL YOU'VE GOT!' Both of them laughed, and they got along great together. In '52 Charlie was an All-America tackle for Hobe.

"They did have one little problem between them at Florida. Woodruff would give all the players Hershey bars during halftime for energy, and Hooser didn't believe in candy bars being good for players, and he often told his linemen not to eat candy bars unless ordered to by the head coach. One Monday LaPradd was on campus and had just taken a bite of a candy bar when he saw Hooser approaching. Charlie stuffed the whole candy bar in his mouth, but he wasn't quick enough. Hooser looked at LaPradd with that candy bar in his mouth and just shook his head. After practice for the next four days, Hooser ran LaPradd until his tongue was hanging out. But LaPradd felt Hooser was a great coach."

"After we beat Georgia in '52, we returned from Jacksonville on a bus," Brannon said. "Sammy Oosterhoudt told me he had a bottle of liquor for the two of us to drink when we got back to Gainesville. Hooser somehow had an idea what was going on, and he didn't like it. We got off the bus, and he walked up to me and said, 'Get into your dorm room right now or I'm sending you home tomorrow.' I went to my room."

Edmonds and Brannon shared the telling of the next story. "Nobody had any money," Brannon said, "and the players stocked up on athletic department T-shirts and jock straps. Once they loaded a van with jock straps and intended to sell all of 'em to somebody."

"All John Hammock (a letterman lineman in '51 and '52) wore were athletic department T-shirts," Edmonds said. "Sarge Bannister was the equipment manager, and he knew what was going on. One day after the players had all the T-shirts and jocks cleaned, Sarge went into their rooms and took all of 'em back. The complaint I heard the most from the players about that was the T-shirts and jocks were clean when Sarge took 'em back but had been dirty when the players swiped 'em."

"Did you ever hear of another team where one of the players owned the most popular bar in town?" Brannon asked. "Sammy Oosterhoudt (letterman half-back, '50, '51 and '52) won the 400 Club in a poker game. Gainesville didn't have any legal liquor then, and the 400 Club out 13th Street, south of town just across the county line, was a thriving place. Sam ran it for a semester, and Edmonds and I worked for him as bartenders during that time."

And Brannon remembered another story: "In '51 Vanderbilt was coming to town, and they really wanted to beat us because of our upset victory up there the year before. We were studying film during the week, and Red Mitchum picked up that Vandy's left tackle tipped off whether the play was a run or a pass—every down. You hear some people say Mitchum wasn't a real football player, but he was, and he was smart. The left tackle leaned forward before the snap if it was a running play.

"Everything was going well for us, and we were ahead 19-0. Woodruff said at halftime, 'Don't anybody hurt that left tackle.' Early in the third quarter the Vandy left tackle got hurt. Woodruff was hot. After that it was an even game. We won, 33-13."

Joe D'Agostino, the All-SEC guard, was contacted right after I visited with Brannon and Edmonds, and he added to their block of stories about that era. D'Agostino owned a popular restaurant in Orlando for years, but in early 2001 he was recovering from his ninth knee operation and living in New Smyrna Beach. He sounded cheerful on the phone.

"Man, did we do some crazy things back then," he said. "That time I put the dead rattlesnake in Casares' bed, he flipped his knife at me as I ran out the door, and it knicked me in the back—nothing serious. He felt bad about that.

"He and I put an alligator into the university swimming pool one night, and it caused a lot of excitement the next day. We got away with it, although they probably suspected who did it.

"Dan Hunter (letterman tackle, '50 through '53) had a .45 automatic, and he had it out one day, and Rick went upstairs and got his Lugar, and it looked like it was going to be a real shootout. Dan began to worry a little bit, and he jumped into the dempsey-dumpster near the dorm, and Rick pumped several shots into it, knowing it wouldn't hurt anything. But it kept people loose around that dorm."

20

James Bates the Gator

James Bates, Gator linebacker in '93, '94, '95 and '96, didn't follow his mother and father, Jim Bates, to the University of Tennessee, the alma mater of both of James' parents. His mother very much wanted him to follow her and his dad to Tennessee, and Dad said he wanted James to go wherever he chose. No one can say James made a mistake in picking the Gators when he came out of Sieverville, Tennessee, High, not far from Knoxville, home of the Vols. For his four seasons in the Gator uniform, James won four SEC championship rings, one national championship ring, honors as a first team All-SEC selection and was elected one of the cocaptains of the national championship team.

"My mother had no doubts that I should go to Tennessee," Bates, presently a Gainesville TV personality and an actor with experience in three Hollywood

James Bates, All-SEC linebacker. (Photo courtesy of University of Florida Sports Information)

movies, said. "I was visiting the University of Florida, and Coach Spurrier talked me into committing to the Gators. I phoned my mom from Coach Spurrier's office, while he, Coach (Jim) Collins and Coach (Ron) Zook were standing there, but I hadn't told them I might be likely to get a lot of opposition from home. She answered the phone, and I said, 'I've committed to a football scholarship,' and she said, 'Fine, I'll see you when you get home,' and she hung up. She assumed I was calling from Knoxville, just up the road. I didn't want the coaches to know my mother hung up on me so quickly, so I kept chatting away into the dead phone for almost a minute before saying goodbye.

"Later, Coach Spurrier came to Sieverville for the official signing. I'd told him by then that my mother was opposed to me going to Florida. We were getting ready to go into the house, and I told him, 'You might be going into a dangerous war zone here.' But Coach Spurrier is so confident of his personality and recruiting skills, he said, 'Everything will be OK.' We went in there, and he gave my mother a big wave and said, 'It's great, isn't it, that your son is going to be a Florida Gator?' My mother said, 'Don't say that. If I had my way you wouldn't even be inside this house.' But she warmed up to the idea eventually, and she became a Gator fan all the time I was here. She wore Florida's orange and blue and everything. But as soon as I finished at Florida, she went back to being for Tennessee and the Big Orange."

Spurrier has often credited Bates with being a great leader on the '96 national championship team by example and by occasional humor that kept the players loose at the right time.

"He didn't always find me so humorous," Bates said. "We were practicing one Halloween, and I fixed up a helmet with a ghoul's mask on it and wore it to practice. We were still doing calisthenics when Coach Spurrier walked by me and said, 'When we get through with this drill, that helmet needs to be gone.'"

People used to get Bates and Heisman Trophy winner Danny Wuerffel mixed up often. They were recruited the same year and played together the same four years. Sometimes an out-of-town sports writer would ask Bates his views on the Heisman Trophy race and the latest offensive trends. James would answer the questions, but there's no record that he ever let Wuerffel's name be connected with anything idiotic. "I never could see the resemblance," Bates said, "until I got through playing, and my weight went down from about 230 to 200."

It was announced at the Sugar Bowl game after the '96 season, when Florida beat FSU 52-20 for the national championship, that Bates had a concussion and would spend the second half in the Gator dressing room.

"It wasn't actually as bad as everyone thought," Bates said. "I didn't stay in the dressing room the whole second half. Early in the third quarter they let me come back out to watch the game. I didn't like to eat much the day of the game, and that was such a late kickoff, I wasn't feeling well from the start. Then I got knocked out, and the way I was acting they checked me to see if I was diabetic. My wife was a swimmer at the University of Florida, and I knew how swimmers get ready for a big meet. They shave all the hair off their bodies the day before the meet. So I did that the day before the Sugar Bowl. The day after the Sugar Bowl, my whole body broke out in a rash, and I had headaches. But I was OK a couple of days later."

Bates hasn't decided which of several possible careers to pursue, but he's taking a shot at TV, radio and the movies.

"In every movie or TV film I've been in, I've got my butt kicked or been shot in all of 'em except one," Bates said. "In that one I'm an airport policeman, and I'm supposed to come through OK. I catch a crook with a bag of dope, and I'm supposed to cut open the bag, and I have trouble with it and wind up cutting my hand real bad. The one scene where I'm supposed to survive, they wind up having to clean up all that blood."

21

The Pancoast Letter

Fred Pancoast, a former University of Tampa quarterback, was a Gator assistant coach, '64 through '69, and he was the offensive coordinator of the record-breaking Gator team of '69 (the Reaves-Alvarez sophomore season). Before that, he was head coach at Tampa two years, and after UF he was offensive coordinator two years at Georgia and head coach three years at Memphis State and four years at Vanderbilt.

When Pancoast got his first head coaching job at Tampa, he was young and green and anxious to be accepted by older members of the coaching fraternity. The last thing he wanted to do was create the impression with older coaches that he was a flake or a hot dog.

But that's the way he came across after he told his secretary to get a form letter out of the file and send a copy of it to John Vaught, legendary Ole Miss head coach. Tampa was proud to get on the Ole Miss schedule when Vaught agreed to a game for October 15, 1963, at Oxford. Pancoast's secretary was also new on the job, and she sent the wrong form letter to Vaught. Instead of one in which Tampa was the visiting team, she sent one in which Tampa was the home team.

The letter from Pancoast to Vaught read in part: "For the game of October 15, 1963, the University of Tampa will notify you what kind of football will be used. The University of Tampa will notify you what color jerseys each team will wear. The University of Tampa will notify you what time the kickoff will be. The University of Tampa will choose the officials to work the game and will notify you who they are."

Vaught did a slow burn when he received the letter, and he sent Pancoast a reply reading something like this: "There is obviously some misunderstanding regarding the terms of our scheduled football game of October 15, 1963. Ole Miss will notify YOU what kind of football will be used. Ole Miss will notify YOU what color jerseys each team will wear. Ole Miss will notify YOU what time the kickoff will be. Ole Miss will choose the officials and will notify YOU who they are."

Bet on it that of the two, Vaught's letter was correct.

Vel Heckman, letterman UF tackle in '56, '57 and '58 and an All-America and All-SEC selection in '58, wasn't much of a fun guy to the opponents who played across from him, but he had an active sense of humor, and his partner in one prank will surprise some people.

"Don Fleming, Bernie Parrish and I caught a 5-and-a-half-foot alligator one night," Heckman said, "and we put him in the trunk of the car. The next morning we told Coach Woodruff at breakfast about it and asked him what we ought to do. He said, 'Let's take it over to the training room and put it in the whirlpool.' Coach saw that Sam Lankford, our trainer, was finishing up breakfast, and he knew Sam would go over to the training room in the next few minutes.

"We had the gator's mouth taped shut, and we dragged him into the training room and tossed him into the whirlpool and got out of there. Coach Woodruff helped us drag him into the whirlpool. Sam got there a few minutes later, and we crept up to the door and watched him. That gator came out of the whirlpool with a big growl, and Sam was gone from that room in two seconds. He didn't know the gator's mouth was taped shut, but he didn't wait to find out. Woodruff laughed louder than anyone that day."

On another occasion during his playing days, Heckman didn't get any chuckles out of Woodruff. "The coaches gave us the same scouting report every week, no matter who our opponent was," Heckman said. "They were always saying our opponent was great on defense, great on offense. Before the Auburn game, the coaches were telling us how great Auburn was in every area. I raised my hand and said, 'If they're THAT tough, why should we even play 'em?' The coaches didn't care for that."

"In '58 we lost to LSU, the national champion that year, 10-7, and the next week we were playing Auburn," Heckman said. "Auburn had been the national champion in '57 and had another undefeated team in '58. Those were the days when everybody played both ways, offense and defense. We had two tackles hurt, so I went to Coach Woodruff's office and told him it would be OK with me for me to play with the first and the second teams against Auburn. He thought about it for a minute and said, 'No, that would be too much. Forget about that.'

"The next day at practice Coach Woodruff called me over during a break and said, 'We'd like to play you on the first two teams Saturday. Do you think you could handle that?' He already knew I'd say yes.

"Against Auburn I played right tackle on offense and left tackle on defense with the first team, and I played left tackle on offense and right tackle on defense with the second team. Auburn beat us, 6-5, but I had a good day. After the game Shug Jordan (Auburn coach) said Woodruff did a smart thing playing me with the first two teams, and he said Auburn really got messed up when Woodruff kept shifting me to different sides of the line. I think that game helped me a lot on making All-America."

"On Mondays, the third team and the redshirts would scrimmage on the practice field," Heckman said.

"Clayton Pickels was running the ball and got knocked out of bounds really hard. Some spectator had left some chicken bones on the sideline right where Clayton fell, and Clayton picked up the bones and laid 'em on his chest and lay still like he was knocked out. Sam Lankford, the trainer, ran over there to look at him and saw all those bones and yelled back to Woodruff, 'He looks like he's hurt pretty bad! He's got some broken bones, and I don't even know what part of the body they're from!' Clayton jumped up and held the chicken bones in the air, and everybody started laughing."

"In '59 I was a freshman coach and lived upstairs in the stadium dorm," Heckman said. "I came home one night, and looking out the window I noticed someone climbing up the huge tower outside. I went outside and waited for the person to finish climbing to the top and to climb back down. To my amazement it was Bruce Culpepper, center on the freshman team. He was one of the smartest people on the team.

"I asked him what was he doing, and he said, 'Coach, I just wanted to see how high it was.' He said he found out it was plenty high, and he'd never be tempted to try it again."

Heckman thought a lot of Bernie Parrish, a Gator halfback in '56 and '57 and later captain of the world champion Cleveland Browns and a Pro Bowl player. "Bernie left after his junior season to play professional baseball," Heckman said (Parrish later switched to pro football). "If he'd have stayed in '58 we might have won it all. We were 6-3-1, but our losses were by one point, three points and seven points. If we'd had Bernie, we might have won every game.

"*Sports Illustrated* came down in the spring and took a picture of Bernie and me, and they said they planned to run it on the cover of the magazine in the fall. Well, Bernie was gone by the fall, so my picture never got on the cover of *Sports Illustrated*. We've stayed buddies over the years, but I've reminded him sometimes of what he cost me."

22

Pace, Staying Alive

No one should have been surprised when Dick Pace became a Southeastern Conference official in both football and basketball. He was a three-sport athlete with the Gators (football, basketball and baseball) during his college days. He was a two-year letterman halfback in football (1946 and '50) after starting college as a 17-year-old freshman in July of 1946. That was when freshman classes were large all over the country immediately after WWII, including numerous 24-year-old veterans.

"We started practice in July," Pace said, who has owned an insurance business for many years in Maitland, near Orlando, "and we practiced twice a day until September. It was hotter than blue blazes, and the 17-year-olds were scared to death. They wouldn't let you drink water at practice in those days, and we'd pray for rain, so we'd be able to lap up the water off the ground. I weighed 155 pounds, and we got the hell beat out of us. The only way we survived was we had a little speed. All of us were hoping we'd get a hurt knee or ankle so we could sit in the whirlpool and miss practice. They only let us take three or four hours of classes in the summer. We were there mainly for football.

"We had a new coach in Bear Wolf. I lived on the fourth floor in Murphree Hall, and we lived three to a room, with one bathroom per floor. There were a lot of sociological differences among the players. We had one player who'd never lived indoors before, and he'd spit on the floor whenever he felt like it. If you got up in the night to go to the bathroom, you'd have to be extra careful or you'd step in where he'd spit.

"After all that, we went 0-9 that year. Our first game was against Ole Miss in Jacksonville. They had Charley Conerly and Ray Poole, and they beat us, 13-7. Ray Poole hit me on the knee, and after that I was on crutches for awhile.

"The football players could sign for their meals at the cafeteria, so we'd take our buddies, the non-players, through the chow line with us and sign for the meals. If the coaches asked you why your cafeteria bill was so high, you'd just say you had a big appetite. Nobody had any money, and there was sort of a family atmosphere in the dorm. We'd congregate in the evenings. Even then Red Mitchum was a good entertainer, strumming matchbooks and singing and telling jokes. Our greatest pasttime was lobbing coins at a line—the one closest to the line would win the coins."

Laughs were difficult to come by and were no fun for their victims. "We'd put analgesic balm in our team-mates' shoulder pads and jock straps," Pace said. "They wouldn't recognize it until they were at practice, and it would burn the hell out of them. We bought some flea powder and would say it was to help our feet. The other players would ask us to give them some, and we'd give it to them, and before practice was over they found out they'd been had.

"Things got better our second year of college when the girls started enrolling. But then we found out that most of them had gotten kicked out of Florida State College for Women, which had become Florida State University and had started taking males. But they weren't all bad.

"We borrowed each others' clothes a lot. Red Mitchum would borrow mine, but he was a lot bigger than me. They didn't fit him, but he wore 'em anyhow. They'd cling to him and make him look like a stud.

"At exam time, some of the players would copy off another player's paper. They said they had to because they'd sold all their schoolbooks for spending money. One player stole an exam and sold copies of it to just about everybody in class. He made some good money, but he got kicked out of school and never got back in. It's a wonder any of us lived through those days."

23

The Wisdom of Curtis

Curtis King was asked to say something about Red Mitchum at a banquet, and a videotape of the scene included these zingers by him: "When we were teammates in college, I said to him, 'Red, you might be smarter than me, but I don't feel bad about that. At least I play football better than you. . . . Red, you're getting real old, but you shouldn't feel badly about that. The things you buy now are never going to wear out. They'll still be good until the day you die."

Jack Nichols, ex-Gator halfback, wasn't impressed when it was mentioned that the team's former manager, Maurice Edmonds, had reached the rank of major general in the Army. "I had a pretty good career in the Army myself," Nichols said. "I made corporal three times, and Maurice only made major general once."

In the 1959 Florida-Mississippi State game in Gainesville, the heavily favored Gators were trailing 13-6 late in the fourth quarter. Gator tackle Danny Royal blocked a Bulldog punt, and Gator end Dan Edgington picked up the ball and ran it in for a touchdown. The two-point conversion was in its second year of existence, but Woodruff sent quarterback Richard Allen into the game with instructions to kick the point and get a tie. In the huddle Allen discussed Woodruff's instructions with his teammates. The consensus was the Gators wanted to go for the two-point conversion. College football is rarely a democracy, but Allen called the play his teammates wanted.

Allen lined up as the kick holder, took the snap and rolled out. Perry McGriff, a senior end, was wide open in the back of the end zone. Allen hit him with the pass, and the Gators won, 14-13. In the dressing room after the game, Woodruff received heavy congratulations for the two-point call. He waved off the kudos and said nothing about the conversion. The players were also talking about the play, but their pats on the back were going to Allen. Several sportswriters asked Allen about the call, and he admitted that he had not followed Woodruff's order.

This may be as good a time as any to explain a couple of things about Woodruff. His former players will occasionally comment critically on some of his actions of long ago, but virtually every one who did wanted to go on the record as liking and respecting

Bob Woodruff's 1950 coaching staff. L to R: John Sauer, Frank Broyles, Bob Woodruff, John Eibner, Hobe Hooser. (Photo courtesy of University of Florida Sports Information)

Woodruff. Woodruff sometimes would think about his answer to a question for several minutes, and someone might think he didn't know the answer. But most of the time he would come up with an intelligent answer. There is no doubt in my mind that he was (and is) plenty smart. I always felt that if he was given a very difficult test, he might not come up with the answers as quickly as others in the group, but that if he were given several hours to come up with the answers, he would register an outstanding grade. Like a lot of us, Woodruff wasn't always good on names. I found that out on one of my first visits to UF in the spring of '57.

I drove over from Jacksonville for the state high school track meet and bumped into Woodruff. I mentioned that the *Birmingham News* preseason SEC football predictions were out. After a brief discussion of the predicted standings, Woodruff asked me who had been picked as the All-SEC ends on the preseason team. I replied, "Phillips and Wilson, both from Auburn." Woodruff said, "One of my ends is good enough to be on that team." Having moved to Florida from Louisiana just a couple of weeks earlier, I wasn't familiar with the Gator names, so I asked him the name of his end. There was a long, awkward silence. A few minutes later, it came to him. "Don Fleming," Woodruff said.

That day in 1957, he and I walked over to the pit where the shot put competition was going on. Woodruff pointed at a tall, broad-shouldered young man watching the competition. "That guy there is a helluva fullback," Woodruff said. "Probably the best fullback in the country." I knew the Gators had a good fullback named Ed Sears, but I didn't think he would be described as the best fullback in the country. I waited for Woodruff to call his name, but after a short wait I asked, "Is that Ed Sears?" "Naah," Woodruff said. "He's a lot better than Sears. Shoot, he's better than Doc Blanchard!" Woodruff thought about it a while, then summoned Percy Beard, the Gators' longtime track coach and athletic business manager.

"Percy," Woodruff said, "what's the name of that big guy standing right over there?" Beard glanced at the man, then turned back to Woodruff with an incredulous look on his face, as though he couldn't believe Woodruff couldn't come up with the man's name. "Rick Casares," Beard said. Casares had been a star player for Woodruff in the early '50s and the previous fall had led the NFL in rushing yardage in behalf of the Chicago Bears.

Most of Woodruff's players I interviewed said something like this about their former coach: "Woodruff was the first person to have a vision of Florida having a great football team. He laid the first strong foundation for Gator football, formed Gator Boosters and most of the other support organizations, enlarged the stadium, beat good teams like Georgia, Auburn, Georgia Tech, LSU, Tennessee and Alabama and gave Florida football respect it had never had before. He didn't win the SEC championship, but he got Florida on the road to success."

In '66 the Gators traveled to Baton Rouge and beat Charlie McClendon's LSU Tigers, 28-7. That was the Gators' Orange Bowl championship team, sparked by Spurrier, Larry Smith and Richard Trapp. The Gators had a 21-0 lead at halftime and coasted to the victory. Most of the Tiger Stadium crowd was gone before the third quarter ended.

After the game, John Crittenden, sports editor of the *Miami News*, and I went first to the Florida dressing room, where there was much laughing and gaiety. Then we walked around the stadium to McClendon's office. We were talking and chuckling as we reached the office. Knowing McClendon and what a tough competitor he was, I said, "We need to change to a straight face going in here. McClendon isn't going to be a happy camper." Crittenden agreed.

We walked in, and McClendon was laughing loudly, and the sportswriters in the room were laughing with him. A few minutes later I told McClendon, "I thought you'd be sad about this result."

"Sad?" McClendon said. "Hell, no. In the third quarter when Florida scored to make it 28-0, I told myself, 'Lordy, we're going to lose this one tonight, 50-0. This is going to be the worst we've ever gotten beat in here.' Then when the final score was 28-7, I felt like one of the luckiest men in the world. We were very fortunate to lose to this team by this score."

The Gators' opening game in '69 was at home against Houston, which was picked by *Sports Illustrated* to win the national championship. Houston was loaded, but the Gators had some of the best sophomores ever congregated on one team. The Gators had posted a 6-3-1 record the year before, and the Gators weren't being picked to be successful in '69.

Gene Ellenson, the Gators' defensive coordinator and morale coach, had given the Gators one of his blood-and-guts speeches the night before and had closed by bringing out "The Pledge," a paper he dared every Gator to sign. The paper pledged that every Gator was going to do whatever he needed to do to beat Houston. The Gators signed it, down to the last man.

The next day on the Gators' first possession, rookie quarterback John Reaves uncorked a 78-yard bomb to rookie wide receiver Carlos Alvarez for the game's first score. And then the Gators scored again and again and again. A national radio network called the Gators' radio booth to ask if the halftime score had been sent correctly. "It's Houston 38, Florida 7, isn't it," the New

York man asked, "instead of the way it's been sent?" Whitey McMullen, a spotter for Otis Boggs, the play-by-play announcer, replied, "No, that's the real score. Florida 38, Houston 7."

Gator fans in several surrounding towns were so moved by the early touchdown barrage, they jumped into their cars and drove to Florida Field, arriving at halftime and plunking down their money for tickets, which had not been gobbled up in record numbers before the game. Ray Graves, who was starting his final season as head coach, reported after the game: "The business office tells me we sold several thousand dollars worth of tickets at halftime. That's never happened before."

The final score that day was 59-34, Florida, and the Gators were on their way to a sensational 9-1-1 season.

24

Dr. Cade's Invention

One of the greatest inventions the University of Florida has ever come up with is Gatorade, the thirst drink born in the fertile brain of Dr. Robert Cade. Having originally used the Gator football players as guinea pigs, Dr. Cade's popular product grossed $2 billion worldwide in 2000. It's been on the market more than 30 years, and its gross has averaged more than a 10 percent increase each year.

In the early years of Gatorade, the university and Dr. Cade squabbled about the profits, but that was settled years ago, and it is believed all concerned parties have profited from the product. Dr. Cade and his three associates on Gatorade (Dr. Jim Free, Dr. Alex deQuesada and Dr. Dana Shires) each were recently given a President's Medallion by UF President Charles

Young, who said, "It is difficult to measure the benefit Gatorade has brought UF and will continue in the years to come. The Gatorade story will always be a huge part of UF history."

Stokley-Van Camp, Inc. first bought the rights to bottle it, and the rights are now owned by PepsiCo after a merger. But the birth of Gatorade had more trials and tribulations than many might assume.

"Dwayne Douglas, an assistant Gator football coach, asked Dr. Shires over lunch one day why football players don't wee-wee," Dr. Cade said. "Douglas had played football for the Gators, and he said he'd never wee-weed during a game, even though he sometimes had lost as much as 18 pounds in a game. Dr. Shires was doing a research fellowship for me at the time, and he brought the idea to me. That started us on a research project. We began with two medical students running around the track and us monitoring them and their sweat. Blood samples and sweat tests a short time later showed that football players were losing more than a gallon of water and 25 percent of their bodies' sodium each game, with decreases in blood sugar and phosphate.

"Gatorade was first used on the Gator football players in the LSU game at Florida Field in October, 1965. (Note: Steve Spurrier and Co. won the game, 14-7.) In '66 Jim Cunningham, the Gator trainer, called and said they wanted Gatorade for every game and for every practice. I said it would be too expensive. Glucose, in particular, was very expensive. I gave him a price, something like 25 cents a quart. The team used up to

200 quarts per game. It would cost more than that to do practices because there would be more players involved than in a game, and there were six practices every week. (Note: The price was estimated at about $50 per game and more than $300 per week for practice.)

"Ray Graves (UF head coach) said it cost too much for practice, so they were just going to use it in games. But when practice started, a lot of players were having heat cramps and heat exhaustion. Seventeen players had to go to the emergency room the first day, and seven or eight were hospitalized overnight. One player had to stay in the hospital 13 days. The cost of all that heat exhaustion was more in one day than Gatorade would have cost all season.

"Ray Graves called me himself and asked for the cost on Gatorade. We had refigured the cost by then, and I told him $1 a quart, and he said fine. Gatorade saved the Gators a lot of money. For instance, in '77 in early practice only one player had to be sent to the hospital for heat cramps."

The Gatorade doctors are still convinced, 35 years later, that sources in Georgia were responsible for the Great Gatorade Hijack of 1966. The Gators had a 7-0 record, and Georgia was 6-1 going into the annual Border War in Jacksonville. The winner would share the SEC title with Alabama, and Florida was favored by a touchdown. That was the year Spurrier was destined to win the Heisman Trophy.

"The team's Gatorade was sent over to Jacksonville in a pickup truck with a couple of managers the night before the game," Dr. Cade said. "The stuff was put up in milk cartons at that time. On the way to Jacksonville, a couple of cars pulled the Gator truck over, and a bunch of Georgia thugs jumped out of the cars and dumped most of the Gatorade and stomped on all but 18 cases. Then they got back in their cars and were gone. Brady Greathouse, the Gators' trainer, called me Saturday morning and wanted more Gatorade immediately. Dr. Everett Fouts, chairman of Dairy Sciences, put some together, and Coach Graves had a highway patrolman pick up the Gatorade when it was ready. Florida had led at the half of the game, 10-3, but Georgia came back on them in the second half. The patrolman got there in the middle of the fourth quarter, but it was too late. (Georgia won the second half, 24-0, and the game, 27-10.)

"After that game, Graves came to see me and said he wanted me to assure him that his team would never again be without Gatorade."

From the start, Dr. Cade and his associates took steps to perfect the taste of their product. In one experiment, Dr. Cade took a swig of their concoction and threw up. "We immediately went to the Thirsty Gator (a Gainesville bar) and drank a pitcher of beer, and I felt fine," Dr. Cade said with a mischievous smile. "We concluded that our great discovery of that one day was that a cure for our early Gatorade was a pitcher of beer from the Thirsty Gator."

In '65 the Gator freshman team and B team were matched in practice in an experimental contest to see how much Gatorade might help. The freshmen were using it, and the B team wasn't. At the half the B team had a 14-0 lead. But the frosh kept swigging the Gatorade, and when the day was over, the frosh had a 35-14 victory.

Dr. Cade remembers: "Larry Rentz, the freshman team's quarterback, shouted, 'Let's play another half!' Several of the B teamers growled, 'Go to hell!'"

That first year for the LSU game, three varsity starters were designated to test the Gatorade: Jim Benson, offensive guard; Larry Gagner, defensive tackle; and Bruce Bennett, safety. The temperature was announced as 110 degrees on Florida Field. Dr. Cade recalled that Benson and Bennett gave Gatorade's taste a good report, but "Gagner said, 'This tastes like piss!' and poured it over his head. I tasted it and thought it wasn't bad, but I said, 'Well, I've never tasted piss.' After the game I went over to the office and took a test tube and pissed a few drops into it. I tasted it, and it didn't taste anything like Gatorade. Gatorade tasted much better." Inventors don't always have an easy life.

Dr. Cade had another object lesson to pass on: "One week we had two players per day to take part in experiments regarding Gatorade. The first day they were Jim Yarbrough and George Dean. Part of the deal was I would buy dinner for the players each night after practice. Yarbrough ordered a sirloin for two, and then Dean ordered one, too. Each night that week it was the same: The players each ordered a sirloin for two. Steaks weren't too expensive then, and the 10 steaks cost me $110, total. The materials we used that week came to $44.

The total experiment cost $154 for a very productive week. What that proves is the cost of an experiment is whatever you want to make it."

Bruce Bennett (Photo courtesy of University of Florida Sports Information)

25

Governor on the Field

When Georgia prepared to attempt a field goal against the Florida Gators in 1969, the referee signaled timeout a split second before the ball was snapped, even though not a player on either team appeared to have called for a timeout. Georgia's kick was good, but it had to be done over, and no one in the press box or on the sideline had any idea why. Still, the kick was re-done, and the second kick, from the exact same distance, was no good. When the game ended, the importance of that do-over field goal was apparent to all: The score was 13-13.

After the game the referee explained the reason for the timeout: "Governor on the field." Florida Gov. Claude Kirk had been on the sideline and to get a better view of the kick he had run on the field just before the snap. The rulebook included a passage about nonparticipants being kept off the field, so the referee's action had been the correct one. A lot of people laughed about "governor on the field," but it wasn't funny to Georgia Coach Vince Dooley and Athletic Director Joel Eaves.

Before the 1971 Florida-FSU game in Gainesville, the Seminoles had a 5-0 record, while the Gators' slate read 0-5. Naturally, FSU was a prohibitive favorite. The night before the game, Florida senior tailback Tommy Durrance, one of the team captains, asked the team to follow him from the athletic dining hall onto Florida Field.

There in the darkness on Florida Field, with the players assembled all around him, Durrance made a stirring talk about how the Gators HAD to throw aside negative feelings on Saturday and, somehow, upset the Seminole apple cart. FSU had won just two of 13 meetings with the Gators to that point, but this was supposed to be a cakewalk.

Durrance had a lot of audacity and was evidently a convincing speaker, too. The next day the final score was: FLORIDA 17, FLORIDA STATE 15.

The next year in Tallahassee the scene was similar. The records weren't as one-sided as the year before, but FSU, ranked No. 13 in the nation, was a 17-point favorite and not many were picking the Gators, who were unranked. A hard-hitting Gator defense, led by linebackers Fred Abbott and Ralph Ortega, knocked the Seminoles loose from the ball a half dozen times, and a former junior college basketball player named Nat Moore ran wild for the Gators. Final score: FLORIDA 42, FLORIDA STATE 13. It was to be 1977 before the Seminoles finally picked up victory No. 3 over the Gators.

The Gator coaches were hard at work preparing for their 1976 date against Texas A&M in the Sun Bowl. The Aggies had a powerful wishbone offense, while the Gators (though owning an 8-3 record) had been weaker than usual that season on defense.

Then the Gator coaches picked up a tendency from watching Texas A&M on film. The Aggies' outstanding 275-pound fullback, Mike Woodard, would lean forward in the Aggies' wishbone if a running play was coming up and would lean back on his haunches if it was to be a passing play. There were no exceptions. Without realizing it, Woodard was getting a head start straight ahead on the running plays and was similarly getting a head start dropping back to block on pass plays, and the Gator defense, to a man, was going to be getting a head start with him.

Alas, the Aggie offense STILL had its way with the Gator defense most of the day. A&M outrushed the Gators, 241 yards to 172 yards, and outpassed them, 122 yards to 58. Woodard was especially unstoppable, running the ball 25 times for 124 yards and scoring three touchdowns, two on runs of one and four yards and one on a pass reception of 15 yards. The final score was 37-14.

The Gator coaches were understandably down after the game. They had gone up against Aggie Coach Emory Bellard, the inventor of the wishbone offense, and they had thought they had a piece of information that would allow their troops to make a top-grade showing. One of the Gator coaches said, "Coming up with those tendencies didn't do us a dadgum bit of good."

But a consensus of the UF coaches after the game took a more cheerful approach: "We were VERY lucky to have come up with the tendencies that we did. Otherwise, we might have gotten beat 75-14!"

In the '86 Florida-FSU game in Tallahassee, the Seminoles hoped to end a five-game losing streak to the Gators. The Gators' best weapon going in was the passing of Kerwin Bell and the receiving of Ricky Nattiel. The Seminoles' top weapon was the defensive play of cornerback Deion Sanders.

The most talked about quotes all week had been those of Sanders. "My teammates think I'm God," Deion said. "I haven't corrected them, because if our opponents also think I'm God, it will help us win the game . . . . Some people refer to Ricky Nattiel as the Gators' No. 1 weapon, but there's no way he's going to catch any big passes Saturday night because I'm going to shut him flat down. I'm going to ride to the game in a limousine, just so I can save all my strength for shutting down Ricky Nattiel. RICKY NATTIEL! RICKY NATTIEL! RICKY NATTIEL! Poor Ricky Nattiel."

Saturday night with a few minutes to play, FSU led the Gators, 13-10, and the rain was so heavy, at times it was difficult to see the field. But Kerwin Bell threw a 22-yard pass into the end zone, and Nattiel caught the ball behind Deion Sanders for the touchdown. Final score: Florida 17, FSU 13.

Norm Froscher was covering the FSU dressing room for the *Gainesville Sun* after the game, and he reported when he returned: "I asked Deion if he had a higher opinion of Nattiel now, and all he said was: 'RICKY NATTIEL! (Cuss words!) RICKY NATTIEL! (Cuss words!) RICKY NATTIEL! (Cuss words!).' That's at least a little different from what he said before the game."

I believe if you polled all Gator fans about their favorite Florida-FSU games, the top two votegetters would be the Sugar Bowl after the '96 season and the '97 meeting in Gainesville. In the first one, FSU came in No. 1, the Gators No. 4, and the Gators won, 52-20, and claimed the national title.

In the second one, only the most hard-line Gators held out much hope. FSU was No. 2, Florida No. 10. Coach Steve Spurrier had a chronic quarterback problem much of that season, which he solved in the FSU game by alternating Noah Brandise and Doug Johnson on every play. It was Spurrier at his brassy best. One of the great adages in football is you can't alternate quarterbacks, particularly on every play. But Spurrier did it . . . against the nation's No. 1 defense. After a soul sapping battle, FSU led 29-25 with just over a minute to play, and the Gators had the ball on their own 20-yard-line. A Johnson-to-Jacquez Green pass picked up 58 yards, and two Fred Taylor runs got the final 22 yards, and the Gators had a 32-29 victory.

If you say that doesn't qualify as a humorous story, how come any time a Gator supporter sees a film of those last three offensive plays, he breaks into uproarious laughter?

Jacquez Green (Photo courtesy of University of Florida Sports Information)

26

Spurrier's First Year

Gator Coach Steve Spurrier, when asked about humorous things that have happened in his Gator career, picked a couple of items from his first year as Gator coach. "Willie O'Neal had worked out my first contract for me," Spurrier said, "and he sent me over to talk to Keith Austin, my CPA, about some of the things I should do with the money. Keith said, 'You've got a real good contract. We should take full advantage of that. I'd like to see you save all that money,' which at that time was about 350 (thousand dollars) a year. And he said, 'If we save almost all of it, you'll be in pretty good shape even if you don't get another contract.'

"Well, that was actually good advice, but I said, 'Mr. Austin, you don't think I'm going to make it as Florida's coach, do you? You think I'm going to be gone by the time this contract is over, don't you?' At that

Head Coach Steve Spurrier did better than expected. (Photo courtesy of University of Florida Sports Information)

time, I thought we were going to win, but a lot of people
thought Florida was never going to be great. Considering the success Florida had had before that time, you
couldn't really blame them.

"The first season we started out 2-0, and then we
got a summation from the NCAA about some charges
against us about rules violations (by the former coaching staff). The NCAA said we wouldn't lose any schol-
arships or several other things, but they said we weren't
going to be allowed to go to a bowl game, and under
the SEC rules, that meant we weren't going to be allowed to win the conference championship. That week
I attended a meeting of the athletic committee, about
25 guys including President (John) Lombardi, who was
in HIS first year here, too.

"The committee was supposed to decide whether
we should appeal the penalty or accept it. Dr. Lombardi
said, 'Obviously, if we win the SEC this year, we should
appeal the penalty and try to go to the Sugar Bowl. If
we DON'T win the SEC, we won't appeal just to go to
the Peach Bowl or some game like that.'

"Some of the people at the meeting asked me if we
had much chance to win the SEC that season, and I
said, 'We've only played two games and only one conference game, but we've already beaten Alabama, and
Georgia isn't very strong this year. If we split with Tennessee and Auburn, we'll probably have a 6-1 conference record, and that will usually win at least a share of
the conference title.'

"Then Dean (Robert) Lanzalotti, head of the university business school, spoke up and said, 'Wait just a

minute! We have never won the SEC championship, and we've played one conference game this year and have six conference games left, and we're talking about winning the SEC this year?' He had a point, and he didn't think we could win the SEC. He knew that something always happened in the past to prevent the Gators from winning the SEC championship, and he didn't think we were going to be immune from the past. So we accepted the penalty, and the players made a vow they were going to win the SEC championship any how, even if they weren't eligible to get the official championship.

"Well, we've won the SEC seven times in 11 years, counting the '90 season, and I always give the players on that team credit for winning the first one. That was the hardest one to win, and they broke through, and now we've won six more titles. We count that '90 title, even though it isn't official in the eyes of the SEC. Our run in the conference has been amazing, considering our past. I still kid Dean Lanzalotti about him not thinking we had a real chance to win the title in '90."

27

Foley's First Year

Jeremy Foley, University of Florida director of athletics, provided a story that was the same incident David Forrester, ex-Gator offensive lineman, sent us, but it was described differently, one from a player's perspective and one by the man who planned the trip. In '77 Jeremy was in his first year at UF, and he was the athletics ticket manager, but one of his most important jobs was to arrange all the football road trips.

"It was emphasized to me that one of my most important responsibilities was to get the buses to pull up as close as possible to the plane," Foley said, "so the players wouldn't have a long, difficult walk the day before the game. The team was flying in to Montgomery on Friday, the day before playing Auburn at Auburn. I went to the Montgomery airport to await the team, and I saw that the gates were locked, and I was told that no buses were allowed on the tarmac. The security chief said absolutely no regarding the buses. I explained everything to him, and finally he agreed that after the plane landed, they would open the gates briefly, and the three buses could drive right up to the plane.

"Well, the plane landed, and the first bus came wheeling in, right up to the plane. And the second bus did the same. Then the third bus came wheeling in and totally impaled the bus onto the wing of the plane. The front exit on the bus was smashed shut by the wing.

Jeremy Foley (Photo courtesy of University of Florida Sports Information)

The bus driver couldn't even get out of the bus! The security chief was screaming at me that it was all my fault, and he never should have listened to me. We had to pile everybody in the party onto two buses for the ride to the motel.

"The next day when we boarded the buses at the motel to travel to the Auburn stadium, the same bus driver was driving the bus I got on! Kim Helton, our offensive line coach, saw him and yelled, 'I'm not riding on this bus! If this guy can't see an airplane, how's he going to get through all that traffic?' There had been some thought in our group that the driver might be suspended or maybe even fired, but he was right back on the job. To get everybody to Auburn on time we had to use him, and he got us there without any mishaps."

Kim Helton (Photo courtesy of University of Florida Sports Information)

28

Remote Control and Kerwin

Neal Anderson and Kerwin Bell were two of the sparkplugs of the '84 and '85 Florida Gator football teams. Those were probably the two greatest Gator squads to that point. Both teams were 9-1-1 and would have been Florida's first SEC champions if UF wasn't on probation. And both players went on to successful pro careers, Neal as a star running back for the Chicago Bears, Kerwin as a quarterback, primarily in the Canadian League, sometimes in the National Football League.

In '84 Neal was a junior, in his third season as a highly productive Gator tailback. Kerwin was a redshirt freshman quarterback who came to UF as a walk-on in '83. He was suddenly skyrocketed into the Gator quarterback job two days before his first college game when senior Dale Dorminey had to surrender the job because of a severe knee injury.

The Gator coaching staff tried to give Kerwin every possible bit of assistance. The first game against defending national champion Miami, the coaches ruled out audibles for their youthful quarterback. (They allowed Bell to audible starting with the second game, and from that point on the Gators were 9-0-1.)

. . . And they gave Kerwin a veteran roommate. . . Neal Anderson.

The sharp black tailback from Graceville, Florida, and the drawling white quarterback from Mayo, Florida,

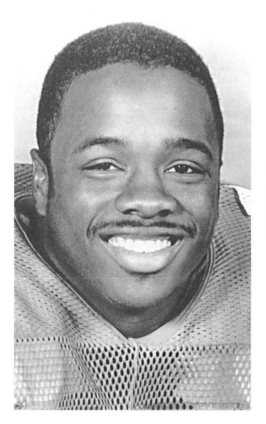

Neal Anderson had Kerwin stumped. (Photo courtesy of University of Florida Sports Information)

may have seemed an odd couple to some, but they became exceptionally strong friends. Seventeen years later, they still spend time visiting each other in their homes. The years that Neal spent the offseason in Chicago, he would stay with Kerwin in Mayo when he came back for UF events.

"Last year when Kerwin was inducted into the University of Florida Sports Hall of Fame, I was there to participate," Neal said. "The first year we were teammates, the coaches wanted Kerwin to room with a veteran player, and they thought I might be a person who could calm him down and keep him loose. On our first road trip, we walked to our room and, like always, I grabbed the remote control and lay down on the bed. Kerwin turned on the TV. He put it on ESPN or some kind of sports program, and I pushed the remote, and the TV jumped to another channel.

"Kerwin put the TV back on ESPN, and I pushed the remote again, and it jumped to the other channel. Kerwin said, 'Gosh, the dadgum TV in this room is broken!' I realized that the remote may not have yet made it to Mayo, and Kerwin didn't know why the channels kept changing. He'd turn it to his station, and I'd push the remote. Back and forth. I started laughing, and Kerwin thought I was laughing at the screwy TV.

"Finally, Kerwin pulled the TV out a little way from the wall, and he lay flat down on the floor and started monkeying with the bottom side of the TV. I don't know what he thought he was going to accomplish getting down there. I just kept laughing, harder and harder. After about 10 minutes I decided I better not let our quarterback get too stressed out over the TV, so I showed him the remote and told him what was going on. I said, 'I guess the remote hasn't gotten to Mayo yet,' and Kerwin said, 'I guess not. I'd say that was the difference in you and me on a lot of things where you know more. I'm a small-town boy, and you're from a big city.'

"I said, 'I'm from a BIG CITY? Kerwin, I'm from Graceville, Florida.' Kerwin said, 'That's a big city compared to Mayo.' I said, 'Man, Graceville isn't a big city compared to anything.' We got to be great friends that fall. We still are."

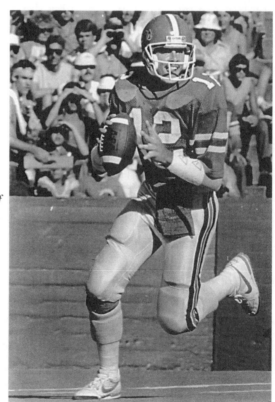

Kerwin Bell (Photo courtesy of University of Florida Sports Information)

29

Graves Had Big Role

Ray Graves was the Gators' most successful football coach until the arrival of Steve Spurrier. Graves produced a 70-31-4 record in 10 seasons. During their previous 26 years in the Southeastern Conference, the Gators had just eight winning seasons and two bowl teams. During Graves' 10 years, there were nine winning seasons and six bowl games. He also recruited Spurrier out of Johnson City, Tennessee, and brought him into the Gator family. Graves was at UF 20 years, 10 as head coach and athletics director, then athletics director for nine years and fundraiser in the president's office for one year. When he left the AD job, he was named UF athletics director emeritus for the rest of his life. He's been elected to the College Football Hall of Fame and seldom misses a Gator football game in Gainesville.

Ray Graves (front) and his 1967 coaching staff: L to R—Don Brown, Ed Kensler, "Rabbit" Smith, Fred Pancoast, "Bubba" McGowan, Jack Thompson, Jimmy Haynes, Linday Infante, Dave Fuller, Gene Ellenson.

Asked if he could provide some humorous stories for this book, Graves said, "Some of the things that didn't seem funny then, seem funny now. Like my salary. I was getting $17,500 a year as head football coach and athletics director when I started, and I'd made more money as an assistant at Georgia Tech because I had some side deals up there. Dr. J. Wayne Reitz, who was the University of Florida president at the time, told me, 'Your salary may not ever be any higher than it is now because the football coach isn't going to make more than the president.' That's funny now when Steve's salary is $2 million a year, and that's more than 100 times as much as the president and the coach made in 1960."

And the coach's salary now is about five times that of the UF president.

"The funniest recruiting story," Graves said, "involved Larry Smith. Every school was trying to recruit him, and nobody could figure out who was going to get him to sign. His mother didn't know, and neither did his dad. Nobody realized that his closest confidant was his 10-year-old sister. One day the sister and I were talking, and just making conversation I asked her where Larry was visiting next. She said, 'Next weekend, he's going to Vanderbilt. When he gets back (to Tampa) from Nashville Sunday, he's going to make up his mind where he's going.'

"The next Sunday when Larry got off the plane, I was there to pick him up and take him home. I was the only coach there that day, and I got him to sign with the Gators." Smith was All-SEC tailback three times ('66, '67, '68), All-America one year and an NFL running back for six years.

Smith, who was 6-3 and 210 pounds, made a 94-yard touchdown run in the Gators' Orange Bowl victory against Georgia Tech, and his pants seemed to be slipping down his hips as he completed the run. Larry's mother, Adele, expressed some dismay to Graves the next time they met.

Graves: "She said, 'With all the money y'all got from the Orange Bowl game, couldn't you afford to buy a pair of pants that would fit Larry?' But Larry had slender hips for such a big guy, and he would leave off his hip pads sometimes when he thought he could get away with it, and that contributed to the pants problem."

One UF disciplinary action left Graves with a chuckle. "After the LSU game in '67, Lindy Infante, one of the assistant coaches, caught Harmon Wages, one of our quarterbacks, out after curfew," Graves said, "and I suspended Harmon for a week. On that first Monday the coaches were running Harmon after practice, and when they got through, I told Harmon, 'I hated to suspend you, but that's the third time we've caught you out late.' Harmon said, 'Don't apologize, Coach. She was worth it.' He had no regrets."

Wages was primarily the No. 2 quarterback for the Gators for three years, then played five seasons in the NFL, most of the time as a starter at fullback. He was 6-2 and weighed from 200 to 220 pounds in college.

"We knew he was capable of starting for us at fullback," Graves said, "but he wanted to play quarterback. I often said if Harmon had come in a year before Spurrier instead of a year AFTER him, the history of Florida football may have read differently. If he had a one-year jump on Spurrier, he might've stayed ahead of him until he graduated. We moved him to fullback in the spring before his junior year, but he came to me after a couple of weeks and asked to be moved back to quarterback, even though Spurrier was beginning his senior season at quarterback and had been an All-America the year before.

"I started to tell Harmon what a tough situation he was up against at quarterback, and Harmon said, 'Maybe Steve will get hurt.' Golly, the possibility of Steve getting hurt was just about the last thing I wanted to hear! But I let him go back to quarterback like he wanted, and he wound up having the best part of his career after college."

Graves had one more unusual memory. "I'd just gotten the Florida head coach job," he said, "and I hadn't even met all the players. I was making some recruiting visits by car, and I was stopping at a hotel in Fort Lauderdale. They had valet parking, and this young fellow was parking cars for them. He turned to me and said, 'You don't know me, but I'm going to be a halfback for you this year.' I said, 'Who are you?' He said, 'Lindy Infante.' He was working at the hotel during semester break, and, by golly, he started three years for me at halfback."

Infante went on to coach on Graves' staff for three years and eventually was head coach of the Green Bay Packers (four years) and Indianapolis Colts (three years).

30

'Friendly Frank'

If there was an award for the Florida Gator who traveled the farthest, hit the hardest, stayed away the longest and returned to Florida with the most devotion to the Gator nation, Frank Dempsey would be one of the top candidates.

Dempsey was a tackle for the Gators ('46 through '49), then an end and a linebacker in pro football for the Chicago Bears ('50 through '53) and in the Canadian League. After leaving football, he stayed in Canada for years as a highly successful gun dealer and returned to Florida for his retirement, now living in Vero Beach as 76-year-old "Friendly Frank."

Dempsey maintains that the most "interesting" part of his life came in the four years he was at UF. He offers several stories of those days and says he left out only the ones that would probably result in the arrest and prosecution of some of his buddies . . . and perhaps Friendly Frank.

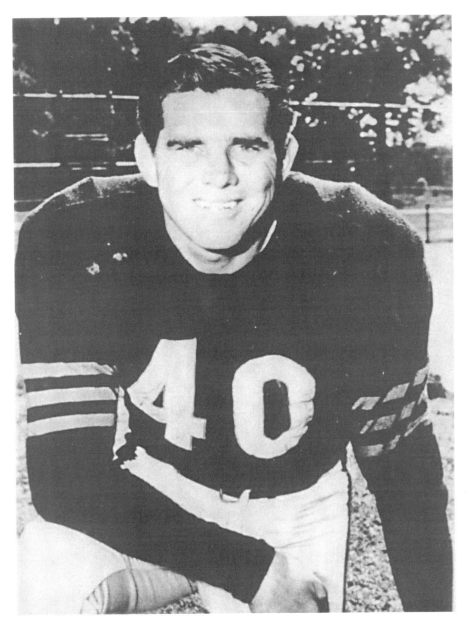

Frank Dempsey kept Dr. Miller busy. (Photo courtesy of Frank Dempsey)

"The football players lived in Murphree Hall," Dempsey said, "right across from the pool and the old gym. There were no girls here then, merely 4,000 bad guys. One night somebody said some of us were chicken if we didn't take off our clothes, climb the high fence to the pool and take a swim. A couple of us did it, and we were swimming in the pool, and all the other guys started cheering and making the most noise you ever heard. And they also turned on all the spotlights. There was only one cop on campus at that time, so we got away. . .

"Now at that time, the city of Gainesville had only two policemen and two cars. I had a jeep that didn't have a top, and sometimes 10 guys would pile onto that thing, and away we'd go. One night I had 10 guys on the jeep, heading downtown. One of the cops pulled up beside us. All the guys jumped off and ran. I stayed and, naturally, I told the cop I didn't know anything about 10 guys being on the jeep. It was his word against mine, so we got out of it. . .

"We had 52 football players, and a couple of them said we should have a candidate in the King Ugly contest at the university. I thought that sounded like a lot of fun, but then the other 51 players said they thought I was ugly and ought to be the football team's candidate. I couldn't dispute a unanimous vote. The votes were a penny apiece. The players got a lot of votes for me, and some of 'em would block the entrances of places where a person could vote; they wouldn't let some of the customers in to vote.

"But the SAE Fraternity boys put up a lot of money for their candidate. They had enough money that they were able to beat me. The players got upset about that and decided they wanted some revenge. There was this big concrete statue of a lion in front of the SAE House. We knew it wasn't going to be easy to steal the lion, so we took two jeeps—mine and Chuck Hunsinger's. (Hunsinger was twice an All-SEC halfback for the Gators and played three years for the Chicago Bears and several years in Canada.) We hooked up those two jeeps to the lion and showered down on the gas, but we didn't budge that thing one inch. All we did was tear up some of the grass.

"So we decided on another tactic. We poured gas all over the lion, then we put tree limbs over that and stuck a match to it. The fire went up like a skyrocket. Fifty players were in on this, and we ran across the street and hid behind a hedge. We had two guys stand up in front of the hedge, and when the SAEs came out of the house, they saw them and started running toward them. Then the other 48 football players came out from behind the hedge and came running right at them. Talk about guys running into the house and disappearing; they were all out of sight in a matter of seconds . . . ."

The football players were planning a blanket party once. One night Dempsey and his buddies were riding around in Dempsey's jeep when they saw a truck ahead of them, loaded with blankets. The truck seemed to answer the players' prayers.

"Now I would never participate in stealing blankets," Dempsey said, "but I wouldn't mind BORROW-ING some blankets. The truck had more blankets than it needed, and we needed to borrow some blankets for our party. That seemed fair. The truck was going slowly, and one of our guys jumped out of the jeep and got the blankets off the truck and onto the jeep. So we now had blankets for the blanket party or cold weather or whatever. I didn't participate in taking the blankets back to their original owner, but I'm sure someone attended to that."

Considering all the mischief Dempsey was involved in, it isn't surprising that one of the episodes backfired on him. "The football players were inducting the new lettermen into the F Club," Dempsey said. "A tradition was to cut the new lettermen's hair off. We took 'em upstairs, and my roommate, Alex Gardner, and myself were acting as barbers. That was fine while there were about 20 or 30 of us taking part, but I stopped once and looked around and realized that Gardner and I were the only veterans still there, and there were about 20 or so new lettermen. I told Gardner we'd be smart to get out of there. The new lettermen realized the ratio about the same time we did, and they started to come after us. Gardner and I ran out and ran to Murphree Hall, where we lived, and blocked the doors, but they got the doors down without much trouble.

"I was on the second floor, and I climbed out the window and dropped myself down—right into the hands of four of the guys who had been chasing us. They gave me a really bad haircut. After they were through, I had to have myself scalped by a barber. I had to go to Miami that weekend to be an usher in a wedding. My girlfriend, who later became my wife, was involved in the wedding, and she wasn't too happy with me. A friend was loaning me a tux, and I thought he wore the same size as me.

"That was another mistake. The pants were three or four inches too short, and the coat was one size too small. I wore his tux, but it looked like I was stuffed into it. That, on top of the awful haircut, made it another day when I wasn't too popular with anybody."

Dempsey probably had more of an acquaintance with Dr. J. Hillis Miller, president of UF, than most people on campus.

"One night I took my Winchester 94 out to the middle of the street," Dempsey said. "At five minutes to 12, I shot it seven times and took off for Murphree Hall. This was more difficult to get away with than a couple of years earlier because the university had four cops by this time. Those shots at midnight in Gainesville could be heard all over campus. I jumped in my bed and pulled the covers up. In a couple of minutes there were three or four flashlights in my face. The cops had come straight to my room. Of course, I hadn't heard anything. 'Officer, it looks like I would have heard that!' Dr. Miller had me in for a little talking to after that.

"I got blamed for a lot of what happened in that era, but my jeep getting several hundred tickets wasn't my fault. The players and students would take my jeep and see how many different places they could put it. Sometimes it would be at the president's home on his front porch. Sometimes up those steep concrete steps in front of the president's office. I was always getting calls, and they gave me all kinds of tickets. Dr. Miller had me over to his office, and he had them bring in my file, which included all those parking tickets that hadn't been paid. There were hundreds of 'em. Dr. Miller looked at all the tickets, then asked me, 'Dempsey, when are you going to graduate?' I think my four years there had been real long for him. I told him I was graduating that spring and next fall would be playing for the Chicago Bears. He said, 'Good. Please try not to get a whole lot more tickets these last few weeks.'

"I didn't have the heart to tell him that after my first year with the Bears I was coming back to Florida the following January to work on my Masters."

Dempsey summed up the stories he had provided: "These things weren't supposed to happen. Lord knows what would happen if I told ALL the stories of those years. They'd probably bring us all back and lock us up, even though I'm a 76-year-old granddaddy."

If Dr. Miller was still alive and president, HE would never ask for Dempsey to be brought back in any capacity.

31

The Brantleys

The Brantley brothers from Ocala, John and Scot, were an outstanding pair of Gator football players, although they were as different as day and night. Once when I was getting out of my car in the Yon Hall parking lot during their playing days, John was walking up to his car. We spoke, and John said, "If you want to see an example of how different Scot and I are, look at this. This is he and I parked next to each other." He pointed to his sports car and to Scot's pickup truck.

John was a quarterback who lettered in '77 and '78, playing close to 50 percent of the time in '77, handling the No. 1 job almost all of '78 and being finished by injuries in the second game of '79. He was about 5-10 and 165 as a college player.

Scot was an All-SEC linebacker, starting four years ('76 through '79) until the sixth or seventh concussion of his career encouraged the doctors to rule him inactive after the second game his senior season. Scot was 6-1 and weighed from 210 to 230. He overcame the concussions to have an eight-year NFL career with the Tampa Bay Bucs. Some thought Scot would hate the doctors who made him miss his senior Gator season when other doctors let him play a lot longer in the NFL, but actually they remained close friends. He used to return to Gainesville to go hunting with Gator Dr. Pete Indelicato.

John provided this story: "One part of college football that no longer exists is freshman football, an experience second to none. The Baby Gators were made up of all freshmen, with some sophomores and juniors who could not make the varsity squad.

"I'll never forget my first college game, which pitted the Baby Gators against the Baby Tigers of Auburn. We traveled by bus to Auburn on a Sunday afternoon for a Monday 1 p.m. kickoff. Stayed at the beautiful Pat Sullivan/All-American Inn in Auburn.

"What a great setting for college football in your initial game as a Gator. Coach Jack Hall, who came with Doug Dickey from Tennessee, was the freshman head coach. My quarterback coach was a graduate assistant by the name of Chan Gailey from Americus, Georgia, a great guy and coach (and later head coach of the Dallas Cowboys and presently offensive coordinator for the Miami Dolphins).

"As we prepared to take the field for the first time as Gators, Coach Hall gave us the pep talk legends would give: 'We're here at a school with tremendous tradi-

Jack Hall (Photo courtesy of University of Florida Sports Information)

tion. The Auburn players are stronger than you, faster than you and we wanted every one of them!' We're feeling good about ourselves at this point. 'Things can go terribly bad in your first game, so don't get down if things don't go our way and keep fighting! Let's go get 'em.'

   "As we run out onto the field on this beautiful fall Monday in the large stadium of Jordan-Hare, you notice a crowd of about 185 people. Barking signals would be echoed throughout the stadium. Baby Gators win the toss and receive. Here we go—Gators vs. Tigers—finally made it—college football—a dream come true.

"As I await the kickoff, Coach Gailey calls our first play, a simple draw play to Alan Williams, so everyone can settle down. Alan runs over me and forces a fumble. Auburn recovers. William Andrews (to be an Atlanta Falcon great) would score two plays later. We get the ball. Coach Gailey calls for a slant pass to Derrick Gaffney. I throw a superb spiral that is tipped by an Auburn linebacker and picked off. William Andrews scores three plays later, but they miss the extra point. Auburn 13, UF 0 (two minutes into the game).

"Remember Coach Hall's speech? He didn't. Walking down the sideline he said, 'Damn, boys, we're gonna get beat 50 to nothing.' Positive thought? The game settled down. We twisted Andrews' ankle and also scored right before the half. AU 13, UF 7, half. The second half, with the crowd down to about 100, nothing happened until the last two minutes of the game when Coach Gailey called the same slant pass to Gaffney but told me to wait 'til the linebacker cleared. Bingo! Catch! Gaffney runs by the safety. Touchdown. Extra point from Trell Brown is good! Final, Baby Gators 14, Baby Tigers 13.

"What a short drive home with the experience of our first college game under our belt. Now, we know what it means to be a Gator. By the way, one of our crafty juniors taped Coach Hall's pregame and halftime speeches. On the bus ride home in total darkness, our 'not-to-be' named player started playing the speeches back out loud. Without hesitation, Coach Hall sent Coach Gailey back to get the tape: 'Chan, I don't care what it costs or how you get it, that tape cannot get in the hands of Coach Dickey.'

"We saved you, Coach. It's in my top drawer in Ocala, used for annual play at our Gator reunions."

At one of the Gators' annual football banquets in the mid-70s, Keith Tribble, a first team offensive guard, told a story on Hall in the coach's presence, and Hall, who has a delightful personality, appeared to laugh as loudly as anyone. Tribble, a letterman in '73, '74 and '75 and now executive director of the Orange Bowl, said he was talking to Hall at the practice field one day about a player on the team who had been a big disappointment as a player and as a citizen.

Tribble, imitating Hall's Southern drawl, said at the banquet: "Keith, you always have a boy now and then that you recruit, and he doesn't turn out well. Joe Jones (note: not the player's real name) has really been a disappointment on this squad. He is SORRY as a player, and he is equally sorry as a human being. Also, (pause), hi there, Joe. How are you feeling? Always good to see you, buddy. (Another pause as Joe Jones walks past Hall and Tribble on the practice field.) Keith, like I was saying, what a disappointment this guy has been. He's just sorry, sorry, sorry."

32

Raising Vinnie

Vince Kendrick was a standout fullback for the Gators ('71, '72 and '73), playing first team the latter two years, then playing two years for the Atlanta Falcons. He was 6 feet, 225 pounds and had good speed for his size. He was an outstanding blocker and a good runner and pass receiver. Occasionally, he broke long touchdown runs, and he filled in well at tailback for several games in '73 when Nat Moore was injured.

He returned to the Gators and served on the coaching staff under both Doug Dickey and Charley Pell. His young wife died during an operation while he was coaching the running backs for Pell. He left coaching a year or two later to devote more time to participate in the upbringing of his son, Vinnie. It was a sacrifice that paid off in superb results. Vinnie played football in high school and two years at Air Force Academy. He made excellent grades, and he's now a career Air Force officer, 25 years old, and he's commander of a missile base in Minot, S.D., which specializes in maintaining nuclear weapons. Vince has remarried (she's a minister) and now lives in Deerfield Beach, where he's director of community services.

⬤

"I had a good career at the University of Florida," Kendrick said. "When Pell came in, he kept me. He hated young coaches, but I learned a lot from him. Pell was a total workaholic. No matter how I tried, I could never beat him to work. I'd come in at 6 a.m., and he was already there. I'd come in at 5 a.m., and he's already there. The first year was miserable. We were 0-10-1. One thing I learned from Pell, we were going to outwork everybody, outrecruit everybody. We all worked 70 to 75 hours a week. He was a true Bear Bryant disciple. He called it working half a day if you worked from 5:30 a.m. to 2:30 p.m. He was always analyzing people and analyzing players. He wanted to run a power-I with two tight ends. He was always on Lee McGriff and me.

"Lee was on vacation once and was relaxing at the beach with his family. He was lying there on the sand, figuring Pell could never find him. A man came running up the beach to him, sweating and all excited. The man had a message for Lee to call Coach Pell right away. Coach Pell had found him, despite all the secrecy. Lee called him, and Coach Pell wanted him to get on this recruit. He considered that an emergency. That's how he was.

"In '80 Coach (Mike) Shanahan came in as offensive coordinator, and he wanted to change the offense to more passing. Shanahan wanted to use four wide receivers, and Lee wanted the wide receivers to get more balls and to get out of the two tight ends. Pell said, 'McGriff, if I'm down in a 3-point stance (like the tight ends), and you're an Olympic sprinter standing straight up, which one of us is going to get down the field first?' Lee said, 'If I'm an Olympic sprinter, I'd win no matter the stance.'"

Vince said, "Pell brought a list of officials to me that were going to officiate our games. He said we'd

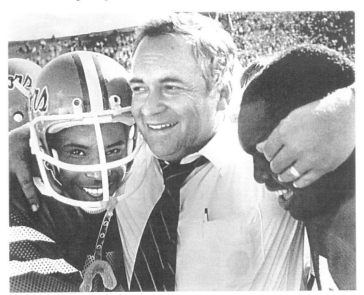

Charley Pell celebrating the 1982 victory over Southern Cal.
(Photo courtesy of University of Florida Sports Information)

have different coaches go up to different officials and ask about their wives and their children, calling all of them by name. He thought that would help us. I did a lot of work on that report and gave all the coaches a copy of it. But when the games started, Pell would have all the officials cussed out by the end of the first quarter, so my report didn't do any good."

"After my wife died," Vince said, "Vinnie and I lived in the players dormitory for a while. The players loved him. I came back from a recruiting trip one night, and Vinnie asked me where I'd been. I said, 'I've been trying to find some football players. That's an important part of my job.' Vinnie starting jumping up and down and said, 'Dad, those boys living upstairs are ALL football players. Go up there and get 'em.'

"I gave Vinnie a pep talk one time that when things get bad, you've got to reach down deep and come up with a decision that will straighten things out. After his sophomore year at Air Force, he decided he wanted to be a top student and be a career Air Force officer, and to do that he decided to drop football."

Asked about his brother, Preston, who was an All-SEC defensive end for the Gators, one class behind Vince, he said, "Preston will never change. When he was playing for the Gators, his fraternity was hazing him, and he beat some guy up, and the fraternity put some penalty on him. Preston thought that was unfair, and he was mad, so he went out on Saturday and took it out on Ole Miss. He had 20 tackles, nine sacks and was named Lineman of the Week.

"When he was with the San Francisco 49ers one summer, I called out there and asked him how he was doing. He said he was getting fined $250 a day. I said, 'What did you do?' He said, 'They're fining me for not eating meat. You know I'm a vegetarian.' I told him, 'When we were kids, our mother was working three or four jobs trying to get us all fed properly. Now you're getting fined $250 a day for NOT eating good meat!' "

33

The Yon Hall Variety Show

Nick Sinardi, a letterman center for the Gators in '69, is now a lawyer in Tampa. Some of his best memories were his playing days . . . and the Yon Hall Variety Show.

"We had one guy living in Yon Hall (the athletic dormitory) who claimed to have a show-business background," Sinardi said. "Mike Olgy, whose claim to fame was that he was an alternate mousketeer in the Mickey Mouse Club. He said we would have a program, which would be mainly stupid people tricks. We staged it in the new locker room in the bowels of the stadium. Mike Kelley (a starting linebacker in '68, '69 and '70) had seen the movie, 'Cool Hand Luke,' in which Paul Newman ate 50 hardboiled eggs. Mike said for his act HE would eat 50 hardboiled eggs. He got the 50th egg down all right, everybody applauded . . . and Mike threw up."

"Mike Warbritton (a letterman tackle in '70) sat down with a tall can of Crisco and ate the whole thing. Olgy said for his trick he would drink a fifth of rum in 30 minutes. We didn't know that could kill somebody, but Mike did it . . . in 30 minutes. Somebody ate live minnows—about a half dozen. It was all in dumb fun. Nobody got hurt.

When Steve Spurrier was coaching the Duke football team (and later when he was coaching the Gators) he used to have ex-Gator defensive coordinator Gene Ellenson come up for several big games to give pep talks to his Blue Devils. Spurrier rated Ellenson the greatest inspirational speaker he knew.

"I don't think we ever lost a game that Ellenson gave us a pep talk beforehand," Spurrier said. "We had him for real big games only. About the third time he was up there, I had 'em bring him from the air-

Steve Spurrier gave Ellenson the Duke game ball. (Photo courtesy of University of Florida Sports Information)

port to the practice field in a limousine. They drove out to the middle of the practice field, and big Gene got out, and the players started cheering. They knew they'd never lose when Gene was there, and they figured it was going to be a big-game victory."

Galen Hall had Ellenson's support (Photo courtesy of University of Florida Sports Information)

Ellenson, at the time, was executive director of Gator Boosters, Inc., and he said, "I'd heard Galen Hall, the Gator coach at the time, had worried to his friends whether I was 100 percent for Galen or whether I favored bringing Spurrier back as Gator coach. I always supported Galen, and I gave pep talks to the team whenever he asked me.

"One night I was returning from a game at Duke, and Duke had given me a game ball with the Duke-North Carolina score on it, a Duke win. I was in the Gainesville airport with this ball under my arm, and I ran into Galen. I tried to hold the ball in a way he couldn't see it was from Duke, but I don't know whether he saw it or not."

34

The Banana Split Factor

Bill Richbourg and Jimmy Hall, a pair of Pensacola products, were teammates with the Gators ('62-63-64), and are now back in Pensacola, where Richbourg is a lawyer, Hall is a doctor, and they're still friends. Richbourg was a 5-11, 205-pound All-SEC nose guard, and Hall was the team's smallish place kicker. They got together, thought about their years with the Gators and came up with these stories for us.

Hall: "Billy Joe James, a Gator teammate from Savannah, wasn't a letterman for the Gators, but he had the highest average in the history of college football: 45 yards per carry rushing the ball. I think he probably still holds the national record. He had two carries, one for 44 yards and one for 46 yards. Billy Joe had terrible eyesight. That's what kept him from playing more for the Gators. He just COULDN'T SEE!

"I asked him how he could see to run as far as he did on those two plays. He said, 'When I break though the line I veer one way or the other, right or left. Then I run in that direction for a while. When the crowd noise gets greater going that way, I realize I'm getting close to the sideline, so I swing back and start running diagonally across the field toward the opposite sideline. Then the crowd starts getting louder on that side, and I know I'm getting close to that sideline, and I change direction again.'

"He wasn't kidding. He couldn't see the blockers or the defenders, and that's how he made those long runs—listening to the crowd."

"That was the truth," Richbourg said. "Real strange but true."

Then Richbourg confessed his longest memory as a Gator player: "When we were sophomores, we played Duke early in the season in Jacksonville. Two other sophomores on the team were Dennis Murphy and Larry Dupree (Murphy was All-SEC second team defensive tackle in '63 and played one year with the Chicago Bears, and Dupree led the SEC in rushing in '62, was All-SEC three years and All-America once. A damaged knee kept him from playing pro football).

"Dennis and I had gotten our ankles taped at the Roosevelt Hotel and were walking around, trying to kill a few minutes before we got on the bus for the stadium. We looked into the restaurant at the Roosevelt, and they were advertising a giant banana split at a bargain price. We'd just finished a pregame meal, but Murphy said he was going to eat a banana split.

"We sat down, and when his split came, it looked so good that I ordered one, too. Dupree came walking in, and HE ordered one, too. We were just dumb sophomores. We ate 'em real fast so we could make the bus and so the coaches wouldn't see us. We got out to the stadium, and the game started. We jumped out to a 21-0 halftime lead, which included Dupree getting sick on an 80-yard touchdown run. You could see on the film later, Dupree throwing up on a Duke player on that run.

"The three of us, the three banana split eaters, all got sick during the game. After leading 21-0 at the half, we got beat, 28-21."

The game was one of the Gators' classic screwups, and few people knew before now that three banana splits played a role in it.

35

An Opponent to Remember

The extraordinary stories revolving around Bill Peterson are enough to get Pete in this Gator book, even if he was never associated with the Gators except as an opponent. Peterson was head football coach of Florida State University for 11 years and got the Seminoles' first victories over the Gators ('64 and '67), which were the ONLY two Seminoles victories until the arrival of Bobby Bowden in '76. Pete coached Rice for one year and the Houston Oilers for a season and a half and finished his career as athletic director at the University of Central Florida.

Pete coached wide-open, explosive offensive football and was one of the leading producers of college and National Football League coaches from the ranks of his assistants. He was a very intelligent person, but he mixed his words up, and they often came out meaning something completely different from what he said. Some people said his voice was just a few words ahead of his mind, but that's for someone else to label, not me.

Charlie LaPradd, the Gator All-America tackle, coached under Peterson at FSU, and he provides this story:

"Somebody had caught a couple of the players smoking. If that's all the players did these days the coaches could be ecstatic, but in the early '60s the coaches felt they had to crack down on them. Peterson said he wanted all the players to be brought into this little auditorium where we had our squad meetings. He said, 'I want the players all sitting down quietly, and I want the coaches spread around the room. If the players talk or make any noise, tell 'em, "No talking! Coach Peterson is getting ready to make an important address." Pete came in and told the players right off, 'Y'all can't put anything over on me because I know everything there is to know. I sure know about smoking. When I was 43 years old, my 17-year-old father died of nicotine of the heart.'

"The coaches started laughing, and we had to run out the back door of the auditorium and roll on the grass to stop laughing."

Eddie Feely was first-string quarterback Peterson's first three years at FSU. Later he was one of the state's greatest coaches, developing a state championship team at Merritt Island and state runnerup teams at Fort Walton Beach Choctawhatchee and Gainesville Buchholz High, and he was on the staff at FSU for two years.

"FSU had never beaten Florida at that time," Feely said, "and Coach Pete called a squad meeting during January before my senior season to talk abut it. Beating Florida was an obsession with Coach Pete. He told us we would beat Florida the way David beat Goliath— by outworking them. 'It's going to be just like David and Goliath all over again,' he said. 'We're going to be just like David. David just kept throwing those rocks, over and over. David lined up a whole bunch of beer cans and coke bottles, and he kept throwing those rocks.'"

David and Goliath happened back in the Old Testament, but it WAS a story with a strong moral.

Vince Gibson, another former Peterson assistant and later head coach at Kansas State, Louisville and Tulane, gives us this one:

"One summer when we were sitting around the office with not much to do, Pete said, 'You know if we have just a fair team this year, 7-3 or something like that, a good bowl game for us would be the Sun Bowl. We'd work 'em hard before the game, but after the game we'd turn 'em loose, and they would enjoy going across the river there in El Paso and visiting Warsaw.'" The

Mexican city just across the Rio Grande River from Él Paso is, of course, Juarez.

Mickey Herskowitz, the noted Houston writer, gives us this one:

"When Pete was coaching the Houston Oilers, National Football League Commissioner Pete Rozelle saw one of their games on TV, and during the National Anthem, several of the Oilers were walking around, talking to each other and chewing gum. Rozelle sent Pete a telegram, saying that if the Oilers weren't more attentive during the National Anthem, he was going to fine Houston a substantial amount of money, and he was holding each head coach responsible for his team's conduct.

"Well, Pete thought about that, and he called his team together for a special meeting about sideline conduct. He told the squad: 'Sunday when we play the Dolphins, during the National Anthem I want each player to be at attention, to have the sideline under his arm and to be standing on his helmet.' "

Pete originated these phrases in his comments to his players:

"We lost the game, but we can hang our heads high . . ."

"Men, you played a terrible first half. I didn't bring you all the way up here on a four-plane engine to play like this . . ."

"Playing Houston last week and Alabama this week is like jumping from the frying pan into the grease . . ."

"Honor is always important in any great endeavor. Like the great American patriot, Henry Patrick, said once: 'Give me liberty or let me live.'"

Butch Lambert, longtime SEC football official, contributed this one:

"The absolute worst football game to officiate was Florida State-Memphis State when Bill Peterson was coaching Florida State and Spook Murphy was coaching Memphis State. There was no way to do your job and not get cussed out. They were completely unreasonable. Spook was still mad because we stopped World War II before we killed every German and every Japanese, and Pete would come running over as soon as we came on the field and say, 'Okay, tell me right now. Are you guys for us or against us tonight?' I would say, 'Coach, we're not for anybody. We're just going to try to call the game right,' and Pete would say, 'The hell you are. You're either for us or against us.' And that's the way he looked at it.

"When Pete and Spook played each other, you knew you were going to get chased back to the officials' dressing room by whichever coach lost the game. I guess the worst thing that could have happened was the game ending in a tie. Then they BOTH would've chased us."

When FSU beat the Gators for the first time ever in 1964, the game was in Tallahassee, and a special interview room had been set up behind the Seminole dressing room. Peterson motioned for the writers to follow him to the room. About 25 or 30 outstanding high school prospects were visiting the campus and were mingled among the Seminole players in the dressing room. Pete stopped several times on his trek to the interview room, shaking hands with the visitors. To each one he said: "Florida State University is going to be the most exciting place in America to play football the next four years. I sure hope you're going to come with us."

Pete's path came upon one particularly sturdy looking young man, and the coach grabbed the player's hand and gave him the same pitch, closing with, "I sure hope you're going to come with us." The younger man looked somewhat perplexed and said, "Coach, I'm Joe Avezzano, your senior left guard." Avezzano has been a special teams coach in the NFL for many years.

When FSU beat the Gators for the first time ever

During one hospital stay, until wife Marge corrected him, Pete was telling visitors: "If I don't start eating by tomorrow, the doctors are going to hook up an RV to my arm."

And once I drove over to Tallahassee to interview Pete during spring football practice.

"I thought we were going to be pretty good next year, but we're not going to be much if we don't do something about this rash pus we've got," Pete said.

I asked him to explain "rash pus." Was some strange new ailment working its way through the squad? I learned that Pete meant "pass rush." The defense wasn't getting after the passer like Pete wanted.

36

Barbara Dooley's Bama Trip

Barbara Dooley, wife of Georgia's Vince Dooley, is a delightful lady. Vince was Georgia's head football coach from '64 through '88 and has been director of athletics since. Barbara told this story during a meeting of the Southeastern Conference schools several years ago.

"In 1977, Georgia was going to play Alabama in Tuscaloosa, and I figured it was going to be the last game matching Vince against Bear Bryant. I wanted very much to see it. One problem was we had a son playing high school football in Athens, and I really wanted to see his game on Friday night. I figured out I could see both games by having a private plane take me to Tuscaloosa on Saturday morning. The trouble was, when I got up Saturday morning, Athens was fogged in, and my plane had to be canceled.

"I knew a couple in Athens that was going to the game, and I called and asked if I could go with them.

The man said, 'You're welcome, Barbara, but we're leaving RIGHT NOW!' I said I was ready, so they picked me up and away we went. We got about to Talladega, Alabama, and smoke started coming out of the car's engine. A highway patrolman stopped to help us and called a mechanic, who came out and looked at the car. He said he could fix it, but it was going to take two or three hours. The couple said they were going to give up on the game and just stay there with their car. I said I was determined to get to the game.

"So I got out on the highway and started hitchhiking. The first car that passed slammed on brakes and backed up to pick me up. I got in, and it was two men, and I was glad to see that both were wearing red and black. They were Georgia fans from Columbia, South Carolina, on the way to the game. The men introduced themselves, and then I said, 'I'm Barbara Dooley.' The driver almost ran off the road, and he looked in the rear view mirror and said, 'My God, your husband is cheap!'

"I told them my story, and we went on to the game. We got there just before the kickoff and walked into the stadium together. Then we separated and went to our own seats. Alabama won the game, 18-10 (and went on to an 11-1 season and another SEC championship). After the game, I went down to the Georgia dressing room, but I knew Vince had a hard rule: no wives on the team plane.

"Vince came out and talked to me, but he said, 'You know you can't go back on the team plane?' I said, 'Yeah, I know.' Vince paced up and down a few times. He was upset with me for hitchhiking to the game.

Finally, he said, 'You can go back on the auxiliary plane with the photographers, cheerleaders and some of the managers. If I didn't let you do that, I suppose you'd hitchhike back in the dark of night and get in the first car that came along, even if it was Frankenstein and the Wolfman!'

"But there's one more chapter to this. The next day early in the afternoon I got a phone call from the driver from Columbia, South Carolina. Somebody had seen us going into the stadium together and had told his wife about it. His wife wanted an explanation, and he said he told her he'd picked up Mrs. Vince Dooley hitchhiking around Talladega and had given her a ride. He said, 'My wife said in all the years we've been married, that was the biggest bunch of bull.... I'd ever handed her.' I got on the phone and assured her that I was the crazy lady hitchhiking to the game. I think that patched things up."

A few years later, a University of Georgia teacher named Jan Kemp blew the whistle on Georgia doing some of the homework for Bulldog athletes. Georgia had to change several policies, and for several years had to forego athletes who could have played before Kemp blew her whistle. There's little doubt that Vince Dooley's football teams were adversely affected for several years. A year or so later, Kemp was sued for alimony by her former husband, and a Georgia judge granted him a monthly payment from Kemp. Kemp refused to pay and spent several months in jail in defiance of the order.

About this time, Barbara ran for state representative and was defeated. I saw a mutual friend and commented, "I bet that was a big shock to Barbara. Has she gotten over it?" The friend replied, "Yeah, Jan Kemp's still in jail, so Barbara is happy as can be."

It doesn't pay to cross the wife of a football coach. They're a loyal breed.